OLD TESTAMENT CHARACTERS

BIBLE STUDY GUIDE

From the Bible-teaching ministry of

Charles R. Swindoll

INSIGHT FOR LIVING

Charles R. Swindoll is a graduate of Dallas Theological Seminary and has served in pastorates in Texas, Massachusetts, and California since 1963. He has served as senior pastor of the First Evangelical Free Church of Fullerton, California, since 1971. Chuck's radio program, "Insight for Living," began in 1979. In addition to his church and radio ministries, Chuck enjoys writing. He has authored numerous books and booklets on a variety of subjects.

Based on the outlines and transcripts of Chuck's sermons, the study guide text is co-authored by Ken Gire, a graduate of Texas Christian University and Dallas Theological Seminary. The Living Insights are written by Bill Butterworth, a graduate of Florida Bible College, Dallas Theological Seminary, and Florida Atlantic University.

Editor in Chief:	**Typographer:**
Cynthia Swindoll	Bob Haskins
Coauthor of Text:	**Director, Communications Division:**
Ken Gire	Carla Meberg
Author of Living Insights:	**Project Manager:**
Bill Butterworth	Alene Cooper
Assistant Editor:	**Print Production Manager:**
Wendy Peterson	Deedee Snyder
Senior Copy Editor:	**Assistant Production Manager:**
Marty Anderson	John Norton
Designer:	**Printer:**
Gary Lett	Frye and Smith

Unless otherwise identified, all Scripture references are from the New American Standard Bible, © The Lockman Foundation 1960, 1962, 1963, 1968, 1971, 1972, 1973, 1975, 1977. Used by permission.

An effort has been made to locate sources and obtain permission where necessary for the quotations used in this book. In the event of any unintentional omission, a modification will gladly be incorporated in future printings.

ISBN 0-8499-8288-X

Printed in the United States of America.

COVER PAINTING: *Samson Pulls Down the Pillars* by J. James Tissot.

CONTENTS

INTRODUCTION

Scriptural character studies never fail to encourage us in our pilgrimage. That is one of the reasons God included snapshots of so many people in His Book. He wants us to see His truth reflected in all these lives—even in the most obscure and unfamiliar individuals.

The Old Testament biographical sketches are designed to help us identify with a few of the ancients. We'll smile and weep, frown and sigh, feel the stinging consequences of sin, and happily rejoice in the victories of various men and women. We will also see *ourselves* in a new light.

This is all part of the Lord's plan. Our faithful Heavenly Father has preserved each life in still portraits for our examination. I encourage you to study each one carefully with me. Stop, look, and listen for those insights that will open new doors of understanding. Don't be afraid to compare. God's Word is a timeless mirror that gives us a true reflection of what pleases Him and what grieves Him.

I am pleased to introduce each one of these people to you. As their lives are unveiled, my prayer is that you will receive helpful perspective and wisdom, which will result in greater stability, a stronger commitment to biblical principles, and a broader awareness of how God works in our lives today.

Chuck Swindoll

Chuck Swindoll

PUTTING TRUTH
INTO ACTION

Knowledge apart from application falls short of God's desire for His children. He wants us to apply what we learn so that we will change and grow. This study guide was prepared with these goals in mind. As you go through the following pages, we hope your desire to discover biblical truth will grow as your understanding of God's Word increases, and that you will be encouraged to apply what you've learned.

To assist you in your study, we've included a section called **Living Insights** at the end of each lesson. These exercises will challenge you to study further and to think of specific ways to put your discoveries into action.

There are many ways to use this guide—in personal devotions, group studies, discussions with friends and family, and Sunday school classes. And, of course, it's an ideal study aid when you're listening to its corresponding "Insight for Living" radio series.

To benefit most from this study guide, we would encourage you to consider it a spiritual journal. That's why we've included space in the **Living Insights** for recording your thoughts and discoveries. We hope you'll return to those sections often for review and encouragement as you continue to grow in your walk with Christ.

Ken Gire

Ken Gire
Coauthor of Text

Bill Butterworth

Bill Butterworth
Author of Living Insights

OLD TESTAMENT CHARACTERS

Chapter 1

SAMSON: A HE-MAN WITH A SHE-WEAKNESS

Judges 13–15

From Greek mythology to Saturday morning cartoons—from Hercules to the He-Man of the Universe—heroes loom immortal in our imagination. And no hero casts such a long and impressive shadow as Samson. His able-to-leap-tall-buildings-in-a-single-bound resumé reads like Superman's: killed a lion with his bare hands . . . slaughtered thirty Philistines who had plotted against him . . . defeated a thousand-man band of enemies with the jawbone of a donkey . . . destroyed the city gates at Gaza.

But just as Superman was vulnerable to kryptonite, so Samson had a chink in his armor through which his greatness was sapped: when it came to women, he melted before his own passions.

Samson's mother may have been a strong center of gravity in his childhood home, but once Samson launched from there, he took off on a misguided orbit that revolved around three women—his bride, a harlot, and Delilah. His desires for these women formed a magnetic field that pulled him off God's course and put him onto a collision course that led to his demise.

Samson and His Mother

From a quiet, yet miraculous beginning to a tragic, yet triumphant climax, Samson's life encompasses all the elements of a Shakespearean drama. Act 1 of Samson's life opens in Judges 13. As the curtain rises, a dark backdrop reveals sinful Israel in bondage to the neighboring country of Philistia.

1

> Now the sons of Israel again did evil in the sight
> of the Lord, so that the Lord gave them into the
> hands of the Philistines forty years. (v. 1)

Against this discouraging setting, a lamp of hope is lit for the nation. Lighting the wick is an angel of the Lord who visits the barren wife of Manoah:

> And there was a certain man of Zorah, of the
> family of the Danites, whose name was Manoah;
> and his wife was barren and had borne no children.
> Then the angel of the Lord appeared to the woman,
> and said to her, "Behold now, you are barren and
> have borne no children, but you shall conceive and
> give birth to a son. Now therefore, be careful not
> to drink wine or strong drink, nor eat any unclean
> thing. For behold, you shall conceive and give birth
> to a son, and no razor shall come upon his head, for
> the boy shall be a Nazirite to God from the womb."
> (vv. 2–5a)

Hope's emerging flame begins dispelling the nation's darkness in the latter portion of verse 5: "and he shall begin to deliver Israel from the hands of the Philistines."

In verses 6–7, the woman tells her husband about the divine encounter. Afterward, he entreats the Lord to have the messenger return (vv. 8–9a). Verses 9b–23 record that second angelic visitation.

A godly, yet somewhat anxious father, Manoah questions the angel concerning the child's upbringing and professional future: "Now when your words come to pass, what shall be the boy's mode of life and his vocation?" (v. 12). Manoah is motivated not by *curiosity* but by *commitment*—a commitment to raise the child so he is best prepared for his destiny.

This commitment is underscored by the parents' anxiousness to make a burnt offering to the Lord in reverential submission to His will (v. 19). In a miraculous display, fire shoots up from the altar toward heaven, and the angel of the Lord ascends out of sight (v. 20). Sometime later, a son is indeed born to this godly couple (v. 24). His mother gives him the name Samson.[1] Blessed by the Lord, the

---

1. Samson is derived from the Hebrew word for "sun" and probably refers to "that which is distinguished, the pinnacle, one who is strong."

boy grows, and the Spirit of the Lord begins to stir in him in a mighty way (v. 25). And upon this act the curtain falls.

From this part of Samson's life we can glean the first of four principles: *Sensuous children can be born of spiritual parents.* A godly, biblical home life is no guarantee against sensuality, as Samson's life will progressively illustrate. He was a child born of prayer . . . who came as a direct result of an angelic appearance and announcement . . . was raised by a family that was sensitive and obedient to the Lord . . . was blessed by the Lord . . . and was uniquely visited by the Holy Spirit. But if Samson's life teaches us anything as parents, it teaches us that even children with a spiritual head start can plunge headlong into carnality.

Samson and His Bride

By the time the curtain rises in Judges 14, many years have passed. Samson is now a virile young man whose hormones boil within him like pent-up steam in a pressure cooker. Unable or unwilling to control his passions, he sees a Philistine woman and becomes obsessed with her.

> Then Samson went down to Timnah and saw a woman in Timnah, one of the daughters of the Philistines. So he came back and told his father and mother, "I saw a woman in Timnah, one of the daughters of the Philistines; now therefore, get her for me as a wife." Then his father and his mother said to him, "Is there no woman among the daughters of your relatives, or among all our people, that you go to take a wife from the uncircumcised Philistines?" But Samson said to his father, "Get her for me, for she looks good to me." (vv. 1–3)

Samson's eyes spur his lust to break the dual reins of his parents' wishes and the Mosaic Law (v. 3; Deut. 7:1–3). Again, in Judges 14:7, as if the Spirit is drawing our attention to the bent in his character, we are informed that "she looked good to Samson."

From this brief episode we gain a second principle: *A sensuous person focuses on the external rather than on the internal.* The first recorded words of Samson are, "I saw a woman." Three times in the passage Samson refers to the Philistine woman in exclusively visual terms. He does not even mention her internal qualities.

3

As attractively carved wood frames a Rembrandt, our external appearance should unobtrusively frame our internal qualities. When a frame is ornately carved, scrolled, and overlaid with gold leaf, it is easy for our focus to shift from the picture to the frame. And this is precisely why Peter warns: "Let not your adornment be merely external . . . but let it be the hidden person of the heart" (1 Pet. 3:3–4). When you look at someone, is your focus on the wood or on the Rembrandt? The appearance—or the heart (1 Sam. 16:7)?

In spite of this maverick's runaway lust, God is *still* in the saddle and *still* in control.

> However, his father and mother did not know that
> it was of the Lord, for He was seeking an occasion
> against the Philistines. Now at that time the Philis-
> tines were ruling over Israel. (Judg. 14:4)

Samson is to fulfill his destiny by delivering Israel from the Philistines—even in his disobedience. God worked through Samson's lust to drive a wedge into the ranks of the Philistines—a wedge so strong that it would eventually cause the destruction of Israel's mighty foe.

Verses 5–9 record an incident in Samson's life when "the Spirit of the Lord came upon him mightily" to help him overcome an attacking lion (v. 6). Later, a swarm of bees hived themselves within the lion's carcass, out of which Samson scooped honey for himself. He uses this incident to pose a riddle to the thirty Philistine companions who had accompanied his bride to a seven-day feast. Bets are placed on both sides, and the riddle is put forth.

> "Out of the eater came something to eat,
> And out of the strong came something sweet."
> (v. 14)

The Philistines are given a time limit of seven days to unravel the riddle. By the fourth day, still stumped, they threaten Samson's bride, getting her to entice him into revealing the answer. After days of pleading and weeping, she finally wheedles the answer out of him and promptly tells it to her countrymen. Just before the deadline, the Philistines answer Samson's riddle.

> So the men of the city said to him on the seventh
> day before the sun went down,
>> "What is sweeter than honey?
>> And what is stronger than a lion?" (v. 18a)

Realizing he has been duped, Samson's rage starts with a verbal accusation and ends with a violent act.

> And he said to them,
> "If you had not plowed with my heifer,
> You would not have found out my riddle."
> Then the Spirit of the Lord came upon him mightily, and he went down to Ashkelon and killed thirty of them and took their spoil, and gave the changes of clothes to those who told the riddle. And his anger burned, and he went up to his father's house.
> (vv. 18b–19)

Hardly in the honeymoon mood, Samson storms away to his father's house. Left behind, his wife is then given to one of his companions (v. 20). Sometime later, the harvest moon begins a tidal pull on Samson's libido. Before he knows it, he's at the door to his wife's room with flowers in hand. (Actually, it was a goat, but that doesn't translate too romantically into our culture.)

> But after a while, in the time of wheat harvest, it came about that Samson visited his wife with a young goat, and said, "I will go in to my wife in her room." (15:1a)

Enter the father-in-law, who stands at his daughter's door sandbagging passion's flood.

> But her father did not let him enter. And her father said, "I really thought that you hated her intensely; so I gave her to your companion. Is not her younger sister more beautiful than she? Please let her be yours instead." (vv. 1b–2)

With thoughts turning quickly from romance to revenge, Samson's rage rushes to fill the sudden emotional vacancy.

> Samson then said to them, "This time I shall be blameless in regard to the Philistines when I do them harm." And Samson went and caught three hundred foxes, and took torches, and turned the foxes tail to tail, and put one torch in the middle between two tails. When he had set fire to the torches, he released the foxes into the standing grain of the Philistines, thus burning up both the shocks and the

standing grain, along with the vineyards and groves. (vv. 3–5)

One act of revenge begets another as the Philistines retaliate by burning Samson's wife and her father (v. 6). In turn, Samson strikes them ruthlessly with a great slaughter (vv. 7–8). Bound by ropes, Samson is given over to the Philistines by his fearful countrymen (vv. 11–13). Again, however, the Spirit of the Lord comes upon Samson, and he slays a thousand of his captors with the jawbone of a donkey (vv. 14–20).

This dramatic part of Samson's life gives us our third principle: *The sensuous life brings one anxiety after another.* The denial of Samson's physical gratification led to anger, which, in turn, led to violence and then more violence. As Proverbs wisely observes: "A hot-tempered man abounds in transgression" (29:22b), and by that transgression a man is ensnared (v. 6a). The sensuous life is baited with enticing honey, but honey is *always* sticky, and the results of indulging in it can be tragic (7:23). Is the bait worth the heartache? Is the snare worth the sensuous step into transgression?

Samson and the Harlot

For twenty years Samson ruled as judge over Israel (Judg. 15:20) and apparently ruled righteously and by faith (Heb. 11:32–34). However, we are told in Judges 16:1 that when he went to Gaza, he "saw a harlot there, and went in to her." Little did he realize that his walk on the wild side would lead him to a snare which would almost cost him his life (vv. 2–3).

This episode brings us to our fourth principle: *Sensuality may be dormant, but it is never dead.* Like embers smoldering beneath the surface of a thought-to-be extinguished camp fire, lust, when fanned in the open air, can fuel a forest fire. And invariably, someone always gets burned.

> For on account of a harlot one is reduced to a loaf
> of bread,
> And an adulteress hunts for the precious life.
> Can a man take fire in his bosom,
> And his clothes not be burned?
> Or can a man walk on hot coals,
> And his feet not be scorched? (Prov. 6:26–28)

Samson's lustful escapades are also graphic visual aids to James 1:14–15.

6

But each one is tempted when he is carried away
and enticed by his own lust. Then when lust has
conceived, it gives birth to sin; and when sin is
accomplished, it brings forth death.

Each snare in this tragic hero's life is tripped by his sensuality,
and like the bird that "hastens to the snare" (Prov. 7:23), it will
ultimately cost him his life.

 ## *Living Insights*

Samson is best known for his hair, his strength, and Delilah.
We know his hair was left uncut because he took the vow of a
Nazirite. But what was a Nazirite? The word comes from a verb
meaning "to separate or abstain." Let's learn more about this group
of people.

Numbers 6:2–21 explains in detail the workings of the Nazirite
vow. As you read through this chapter, jot down the requirements
for being a Nazirite. This study will help you understand the backdrop not only of Samson's life, but also of the lives of Samuel, John
the Baptist, and the apostle Paul.

Verse: _____

Requirement: _____

_____

Verse: _____

Requirement: _____

_____

Verse: _____

Requirement: _____

_____

Verse: _____

Requirement: _____

_____

Verse: _____

Requirement: _____

_____

Verse: _____

Requirement: _____

_____

Verse: _____

Requirement: _____

_____

Verse: _____

Requirement: _____

_____

Verse: _____

Requirement: _____

_____

Verse: _____

Requirement: _____

_____

🍇 *Living Insights*

This lesson highlights four principles for us today. If there is a generation that needs to review these principles, it is ours. Let's take time to do that now.

- *Sensuous children can be born of spiritual parents.* Do you agree?

_____

Can you think of other biblical examples of this principle?

_____

_____

_____

_____

What seemed to happen in the lives of these people?

_____

_____

_____

_____

- *A sensuous person focuses on the external rather than on the internal.* What part should "good looks" play in developing a relationship?

_____

_____

_____

- *The sensuous life brings one anxiety after another.* How does the media downplay this?

_____

_____

_____

Are you aware of specific anxieties being created by a sensual life? What are they?

_____

_____

_____

How can they be dealt with?

_____

_____

_____

_____

- *Sensuality may be dormant, but it is never dead.* Does age have anything to do with sensuous living?

  _____

  _____

  If you don't "outgrow" sensual thoughts, how should you deal with them?

  _____

  _____

  _____

  _____

Chapter 2

SAMSON: HOW THE MIGHTY ARE FALLEN!

Judges 16:4–31

In Greek mythology, Achilles was the son of Peleus, king of the Myrmidons, and Thetis, a sea goddess. Achilles was the greatest, bravest, and most handsome warrior of Agamemnon's army. One of the tales about his childhood relates how Thetis held the young Achilles by the heel and dipped him in the waters of the river Styx. Through the water's mythological power, Achilles became invulnerable—that is, every part except the heel by which he was held. That small portion of his body, untouched by the water, remained vulnerable. From this story we get the term "Achilles' heel," which describes our greatest point of vulnerability. It was at just this point that an arrow struck the near-invincible Achilles and killed him.

We all have our own "Achilles' heels"—points of extreme vulnerability in our walk with God. For some, it's money; for others, ambition. For Samson, it was sensuality.

Samson's Delilah

When Samson left the harlot of Gaza (Judges 16:1–3), he fell into the arms of yet another woman—the infamous Delilah.[1]

> After this it came about that he loved a woman in
> the valley of Sorek, whose name was Delilah. (v. 4)

The valley of Sorek was the place of the "choice red grape."[2] Certain foods connote to us worlds of description. For example, beans and cornbread suggest poverty. Caviar and champagne, on the other hand, suggest prosperity. The "choice red grape" connotes pleasure. It breathes the enticing bouquet of sensuality.

And it was in this hedonistic valley that Samson roamed and picked the luscious Delilah from the vine to be his next conquest.

---

1. The name Delilah literally means "the weak one" or "the longing one."

2. Alfred Edersheim, *Old Testament Bible History* (Grand Rapids, Mich.: William B. Eerdmans Publishing Co., 1972), vol. 3, p. 174.

The irony, however, was that *he* would end up being conquered—not Delilah.[3] Having a good understanding of Samson's weakness, the Philistines solicited Delilah's help to discover the secret of his strength.

> And the lords of the Philistines came up to her, and said to her, "Entice him, and see where his great strength lies and how we may overpower him that we may bind him to afflict him. Then we will each give you eleven hundred pieces of silver." (v. 5)

The Hebrew word *entice* means "to find an opening"—a point of vulnerability, an Achilles' heel. The same word is used earlier when Samson's wife is threatened by the Philistines: "*Entice* your husband, that he may tell us the riddle, lest we burn you and your father's house with fire" (14:15, emphasis added).

The word is also used in James 1:14: "But each one is tempted when he is carried away and *enticed* by his own lust" (emphasis added). Here the Greek word means "luring with bait." It's the picture of a fish nestled quietly underneath a sheltered place, and a cunning fisherman who has just dropped the bait. Whether artificial or real, the bait is designed to appeal to the nature of the fish—to entice. And different fish are enticed by different baits. For catfish, the fisherman would probably use a treble hook concealed in some form of dough bait or blood bait. For trout, possibly a hand-tied fly or salmon eggs.

For Samson, the enticement was the lure of the opposite sex. Like an unsuspecting fish, Samson is drawn in by Delilah, slowly but surely. Naively, the bait is taken, and fatefully, the hook is set. Follow the progression in Proverbs 7:6–23 to see how Samson ended up on Delilah's stringer.

> For at the window of my house
> I looked out through my lattice,
> And I saw among the naive,
> I discerned among the youths,
> A young man lacking sense,
> Passing through the street near her corner;
> And he takes the way to her house,
> In the twilight, in the evening,
> In the middle of the night and in the darkness.

---

3. There is pleasure in sexual sin—at least for a season—but its sweet grapes are quick to ferment and sour. See Proverbs 5:3–5, and 6:25–26.

And behold, a woman comes to meet him,
Dressed as a harlot and cunning of heart.
She is boisterous and rebellious;
Her feet do not remain at home;
She is now in the streets, now in the squares,
And lurks by every corner.
So she seizes him and kisses him,
And with a brazen face she says to him:
"I was due to offer peace offerings;
Today I have paid my vows.
Therefore I have come out to meet you,
To seek your presence earnestly, and I have found
     you.
I have spread my couch with coverings,
With colored linens of Egypt.
I have sprinkled my bed
With myrrh, aloes and cinnamon.
Come, let us drink our fill of love until morning;
Let us delight ourselves with caresses.
For the man is not at home,
He has gone on a long journey;
He has taken a bag of money with him,
At full moon he will come home."
With her many persuasions she entices him;
With her flattering lips she seduces him.
Suddenly he follows her,
As an ox goes to the slaughter,
Or as one in fetters to the discipline of a fool,
Until an arrow pierces through his liver;
As a bird hastens to the snare,
So he does not know that it will cost him his life.

Like the naive young man in this passage, we all have our weak points. It is important to know your strengths. But it is life-or-death *essential* to know your weaknesses. Strengths lead to triumph; weaknesses, to defeat. It was the unprotected heel of Achilles that proved fatal to the mythological hero. And it was Samson's vulnerability to sexual enticement that led to his demise.

What is your Achilles' heel? Is it sex . . . greed . . . ambition . . . selfishness . . . drugs . . . alcohol . . . worry . . . anger? Possibly, like Samson, your area of weakness is a blind spot to you. If so, you can bet the aisle seat that the people around you see your weaknesses on a big screen, in 3-D, and in Technicolor. Certainly the Philistines could see Samson's. Why don't you ask a few friends for a candid film review of your life? Remember that "faithful are the wounds of a friend, but deceitful are the kisses of an enemy" (Prov. 27:6). And be thankful that you're surrounded by friends rather than Philistines!

Judges 16:6–14 records Delilah's attempts to unravel the mystery of Samson's strength in order to weaken him for the Philistines. In verses 6, 10, and 13 she questions him, and Samson gives answers that progressively gravitate to the truth: "Bind me with seven fresh cords that have not been dried" (v. 7a); "Bind me tightly with new ropes which have not been used" (v. 11a); "Weave the seven locks of my hair with the web and fasten it" (v. 13a).

Frustrated, Delilah poses a final question to Samson, whose answer leads to his demise.

Samson's Demise

Ironically, the strongest among men is weakened not by soldiers or armies but by one woman. Samson could break the ropes and cords that entwined him, but he could not extricate himself from the entanglements with Delilah, "the weak one." Samson's cards, which he had held so closely to his chest, are trumped by this persistent woman's final ace: "How can you say 'I love you,' when your heart is not with me?" (v. 15). He folds under pressure in verse 16 and finally reveals his hand in verse 17.

> So he told her all that was in his heart and said to her, "A razor has never come on my head, for I have been a Nazirite to God from my mother's womb. If I am shaved, then my strength will leave me and I shall become weak and be like any other man."

Samson's hair was only an outward symbol of his inward commitment to God. Obviously, the latter had eroded to such an extent that the former was no longer sacred to him. In reality, Samson's superhuman strength lay not in his uncut hair but in the mighty presence of God in his life (v. 20).

The fall of Samson can be traced to two things: (1) he didn't know his weakness, and (2) he didn't know his strength. Mistakenly, Samson doesn't see God as the real source of his strength. Instead, he sees only himself (see 15:14–17). Consequently, God allows Samson's strength to be taken from him so that in painful circumstances he will learn that without the omnipotent God, he is impotent.

As he sleeps, his hair is shaved (16:19). When he awakes, he is surrounded not by the presence of the Lord but by the revengefully cruel Philistines (v. 20). They seize him, gouge out his eyes, shackle him in bronze chains, and force him to the lowest work a slave in prison could do—grinding grain while harnessed to a millstone.

Samson had grown to depend on his own strength instead of God's. In order that we might learn to lean on Him and not on false supports, God removes our crutches—often gently, but sometimes suddenly and without warning. This is exactly what He did with Samson.

What about you? Are you trusting in something other than God for your safety, your security, your strength? Possibly you depend more on a portfolio or a financial statement. If so, maybe God will take away that crutch—not so you will fall, but so you will learn, as Samson did, to lean on Him.

> The name of the Lord is a strong tower;
> The righteous runs into it and is safe.
> A rich man's wealth is his strong city,
> And like a high wall in his own imagination.
> (Prov. 18:10–11)

Samson's Death

During Samson's dark experience in the dungeon, God's grace begins to glimmer dimly. Samson's hair was growing back (v. 22)! And as his hair grows, so does his relationship with the Lord. Running his hands through his hair, Samson turns his thoughts and heart back to God.

Meanwhile, more than three thousand Philistines have gathered to offer a great sacrifice to their god Dagon[4] (vv. 23–24). For

---

4. It is debated whether Dagon was a fish-god or a grain-god, but we do know that in Palestine he was the principal deity of the Philistines during the Old Testament period (Judg. 16:23; 1 Sam. 5:2–3; 31:10; 1 Chron. 10:10). Archaeological remains lend support to the accuracy of Judges 16:23–31. Bruce K. Waltke mentions an unearthed Philistine temple at Tel Qasile, "whose artifactual remains, including two pillars separated by a space the length of a very large man's arm span and in front of the altar, comports most favorably with the literary description of [Dagon's] temple at Gaza." *Theological Wordbook of the Old Testament*, ed. R. Laird Harris, Gleason L. Archer, Jr., and Bruce K. Waltke (Chicago, Ill.: Moody Press, 1980), vol. 1, p. 183.

entertainment, they summon Samson from prison, amusing themselves with him as he stands between the pillars of the house
(vv. 25–27). Humiliated, he makes a final request of God.

> Then Samson called to the Lord and said, "O
> Lord God, please remember me and please strengthen
> me just this time, O God, that I may at once be
> avenged of the Philistines for my two eyes." And
> Samson grasped the two middle pillars on which the
> house rested, and braced himself against them, the
> one with his right hand and the other with his left.
> And Samson said, "Let me die with the Philistines!"
> And he bent with all his might so that the house
> fell on the lords and all the people who were in it.
> So the dead whom he killed at his death were more
> than those whom he killed in his life. (vv. 28–30)

Like Christ, who selflessly died to defeat His enemies of death
and the devil, Samson, in an act of self-denial, fulfills his destiny
to "begin to deliver Israel from the hands of the Philistines" (13:5b).

A Final Application

With beggar's hands of faith, Samson reaches out to touch the
feet of his God: "O Lord God, please remember me. . . ." (16:28).
If you're an unbeliever, you can pray with the thief on the cross—
"Remember me"—and be assured that you will be with Jesus in para-
dise (Luke 23:42–43). If you're a believer with a burden, you can
pray with the barren Hannah—"Remember me"—and be assured
of His compassionate intervention in your circumstances (1 Sam.
1:11–20). If you're a believer who's blown it, you can pray with
Samson—"Remember me"—and be assured that God's strength
can help you overcome your defeated past (Judg. 16:28–30).

Maybe somewhere along the line you've forgotten God. The
tendency is to think that He, too, has forgotten you. But if the
very hairs of your head are numbered, how could He forget *you?*
Call to Him, won't you? Whether you're a condemned thief, a
burdened Hannah, or a wayward Samson, reach out with hands
of faith to touch His feet and heart with the simple prayer—
"Remember me."

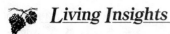

Living Insights

Resisting the lure of lust is a tough job, in fact, it's a battle. And that means we need to know our resources, our weapons, and our enemy's strategy. In Proverbs, Solomon passed on a battle plan to his sons. Let's familiarize ourselves with his wise directives.

Spend some time reading Proverbs 5–7, keeping your eye out for four specific topics: (1) descriptions of the harlot, (2) descriptions of the fool who succumbs to her, (3) descriptions of the wise man who turns away, and (4) practical advice on how to avoid the harlot.

Descriptions of the harlot: _____

_____

_____

_____

_____

Descriptions of the fool: _____

_____

_____

_____

_____

Descriptions of the wise man: _____

_____

_____

_____

_____

Practical advice: _____

_____

_____

_____

What a message Samson could have passed on to his children! We can see many of the same thoughts manifested in Solomon's writings to his sons. Let's personalize these concepts in our own lives.

Write your own version of Proverbs 5–7. You may want to paraphrase certain portions, or you may want to write about *your* feelings as you would convey them to your children. Include such matters as admitting and conquering weakness, trifling with sacred things, taking God seriously, and revealing secrets of the heart.

_____

_____

_____

_____

_____

_____

_____

_____

_____

_____

_____

_____

_____

_____

_____

_____

_____

_____

_____

Chapter 3

ABIGAIL:
A WOMAN OF WISDOM
1 Samuel 25

Hollywood thrives on Cinderella stories with happily-ever-after endings. Deep down inside—regardless of how fairy-taleish they seem—stories like that thrill us because we have this almost genetically coded longing for things to work out happily in the end. A sense of inbred justice causes us to "hiss" Cinderella's cruel and ugly stepsisters and to "hurray" the kind and handsome prince as he sweeps her off her feet. We become wrapped up in the drama because we ourselves are often surrounded by cruel and ugly circumstances. We know how it feels to be on our knees, scrubbing away at heartache until our backs go into spasms and our fingers bleed. Like Cinderella, we long for some charming, princely circumstance to come along and whisk us away from the charwoman's drudgery of life's dirty floors.

First Samuel 25 contains one such script. The lead actress—Abigail—plays an Academy Award-winning part that is the envy of every woman.

The Cast

Chapter 25 resembles a three-act play. Following the cast's introductions is the description of the *conflict* on which the plot is centered, the escalating action which leads to a *climax,* and a *conclusion* which resolves the conflict. In verses 1–3, the three primary cast members are introduced—David, Nabal, and Abigail.

> Then Samuel died; and all Israel gathered together and mourned for him, and buried him at his house in Ramah. And David arose and went down to the wilderness of Paran.
>
> Now there was a man in Maon whose business was in Carmel; and the man was very rich, and he had three thousand sheep and a thousand goats. And it came about while he was shearing his sheep in Carmel (now the man's name was Nabal, and his

19

wife's name was Abigail. And the woman was intelligent and beautiful in appearance, but the man was harsh and evil in his dealings, and he was a Calebite), that David heard in the wilderness that Nabal was shearing his sheep.

The contrast in character between Nabal and Abigail stands out sharply and intensifies the dramatic premise that revolves around the upcoming conflict between David and Nabal.

The Conflict

David and his band of six hundred men looked after the animals of numerous ranchers in the wilderness of Paran, protecting them from thieves and animals of prey. Payment for the service, like gratuities for waiters, was voluntary. No contracts were written; no words exchanged. But it was understood, like the custom of tipping, that at sheepshearing time a rancher was to pay everyone who had protected his animals (see v. 21).

So David sent ten men to Nabal with a tip tray and these words: "Please give whatever you find at hand to your servants and to your son David" (v. 8). The request was gracious and fair in light of their service and protection (see v. 15). Nabal's miserly, penny-pinching response, however, was far from gracious or fair.

> But Nabal answered David's servants, and said, "Who is David? And who is the son of Jesse? There are many servants today who are each breaking away from his master. Shall I then take my bread and my water and my meat that I have slaughtered for my shearers, and give it to men whose origin I do not know?" (vv. 10–11)

Nabal had sheared many sheep, but David would not be one of them. When David heard from his servants how Nabal tried to fleece them out of their just due, he set out to do a little fleecing of his own—*literally!*

> And David said to his men, "Each of you gird on his sword." So each man girded on his sword. And David also girded on his sword, and about four hundred men went up behind David while two hundred stayed with the baggage. (v. 13)

The Climax

Meanwhile, back at the ranch, Nabal's wife, Abigail, was alerted to the situation.

> But one of the young men told Abigail, Nabal's wife, saying, "Behold, David sent messengers from the wilderness to greet our master, and he scorned them. Yet the men were very good to us, and we were not insulted, nor did we miss anything as long as we went about with them, while we were in the fields. They were a wall to us both by night and by day, all the time we were with them tending the sheep. Now therefore, know and consider what you should do, for evil is plotted against our master and against all his household; and he is such a worthless man that no one can speak to him." (vv. 14–17)

Had Abigail reacted like any ordinary woman trapped in an unhappy, mismatched marriage, she might have been tempted to sit back and allow David's vengeance to run its course. After all, Nabal's death would release her from the miserable relationship. But Abigail is no ordinary woman. She steps in, selflessly, to make peace.

> Then Abigail hurried and took two hundred loaves of bread and two jugs of wine and five sheep already prepared and five measures of roasted grain and a hundred clusters of raisins and two hundred cakes of figs, and loaded them on donkeys. And she said to her young men, "Go on before me; behold, I am coming after you." But she did not tell her husband Nabal. And it came about as she was riding on her donkey and coming down by the hidden part of the mountain, that behold, David and his men were coming down toward her; so she met them. (vv. 18–20)

The meeting could have been a fiery clash, but Abigail's humility and honesty doused David's wrath like water on a camp fire.

> When Abigail saw David, she hurried and dismounted from her donkey, and fell on her face before David, and bowed herself to the ground. And she fell at his feet and said, "On me alone, my lord, be

the blame. And please let your maidservant speak to you, and listen to the words of your maidservant. Please do not let my lord pay attention to this worthless man, Nabal, for as his name is, so is he. Nabal is his name and folly is with him; but I your maidservant did not see the young men of my lord whom you sent. Now therefore, my lord, as the Lord lives, and as your soul lives, since the Lord has restrained you from shedding blood, and from avenging yourself by your own hand, now then let your enemies, and those who seek evil against my lord, be as Nabal. And now let this gift which your maidservant has brought to my lord be given to the young men who accompany my lord. Please forgive the transgression of your maidservant; for the Lord will certainly make for my lord an enduring house, because my lord is fighting the battles of the Lord, and evil shall not be found in you all your days." (vv. 23–28)

In verse 28, Abigail's view of God as the sovereign source of blessing shapes her appeal in verses 29–31. The plea softens David's heart and turns it back to God.

Then David said to Abigail, "Blessed be the Lord God of Israel, who sent you this day to meet me, and blessed be your discernment, and blessed be you, who have kept me this day from bloodshed, and from avenging myself by my own hand. Nevertheless, as the Lord God of Israel lives, who has restrained me from harming you, unless you had come quickly to meet me, surely there would not have been left to Nabal until the morning light as much as one male." So David received from her hand what she had brought him, and he said to her, "Go up to your house in peace. See, I have listened to you and granted your request." (vv. 32–35)

Abigail had come to intercede as a peacemaker and ends up leaving with David's assurance: "Go up to your house in peace" (v. 35a). The blessing bestowed on her by God for being a peacemaker far exceeds her wildest imaginings (compare Matt. 5:9).

The Conclusion

Abigail returns home to find her husband holding a self-indulgent feast where he had become "very drunk" (v. 36). She waits until the next morning to tell him of her encounter with David. Once informed, he is seized with fear and falls into a coma (v. 37). God intervenes ten days later: "The Lord struck Nabal, and he died" (v. 38). However, the drama doesn't end on a dismal note, but in a fairy-tale fashion.

> When David heard that Nabal was dead, he said, "Blessed be the Lord, who has pleaded the cause of my reproach from the hand of Nabal, and has kept back His servant from evil. The Lord has also returned the evildoing of Nabal on his own head." Then David sent a proposal to Abigail, to take her as his wife. . . . Then Abigail quickly arose, and rode on a donkey, with her five maidens who attended her; and she followed the messengers of David, and became his wife. (vv. 39–42)

Thus we end our story, as the happy couple rides off into the sunset.

Final Reviews

But what is the critic's review? What can be learned from the drama? At least five things.

First, from verse 3: *Differences between husbands and wives do not mean that the marriage cannot continue.* Differences bring not only conflicts but challenges. Sparks may fly on occasion, but as iron sharpens iron, so one person can sharpen another (Prov. 27:17).

Second, from verses 17–18: *The wife's primary role is to support her husband.* The woman is to love her man and meet his needs. It is God's responsibility to make him good.

Third, from verses 19 and 36: *Silence and timing are two of the most effective ways to handle a strained relationship* (see also 1 Pet. 3:1–2). Abigail's gentle and quiet spirit knew instinctively what to say and when to say it.

Fourth, from verse 25: *There is a difference between harsh criticism and honest realism in relating to your mate.* The difference is motive.

Fifth, from verse 39: *God honors the wife who honors her husband* (see also 1 Pet. 3:5–6). In this case, Abigail was relieved of the strain. In some cases, God gives grace to bear the strain.

As the curtain falls, we feel like giving the drama a standing ovation. Justice is done. Wrong is either righted or forgiven. A bad marriage ends by God's sovereign touch and a new one romantically begins. Cinderella meets her Prince Charming, and we feel assured that they will live happily ever after.

 Living Insights

As we study the life of Abigail, it becomes readily evident that she was a godly woman. She possessed many of the traits that other biblical writers mention when praising qualities of womanhood.

Read through 1 Samuel 25 again, writing down Abigail's characteristics. Then note which of her traits are actually stated as principles in complementary Scripture passages. Such passages as Genesis 2, Proverbs 31, Ephesians 5, and 1 Peter 3 are a good place to start. For future reference, be sure to list the Scripture passage involved after you record the principle.

Abigail's Traits	The Godly Woman's Traits

In Abigail we see a rare blend of feminine ingenuity and wifely support. What a winning combination! If you're a wife, where do you rate in these categories? If you're a husband, how's your attitude when it comes to your relationship with your wife? Do you fit in a "Nabal" category?

Take this little quiz by checking the appropriate box.

1. Differences between husbands and wives do not mean the marriage cannot continue.
   - ☐ Disagree
   - ☐ Not Sure
   - ☐ Agree but Doesn't Apply
   - ☐ Agree and Applies
2. The wife's primary role is to support her husband.
   - ☐ Disagree
   - ☐ Not Sure
   - ☐ Agree but Doesn't Apply
   - ☐ Agree and Applies
3. Silence and timing are two of the most effective ways to handle a strained relationship.
   - ☐ Disagree
   - ☐ Not Sure
   - ☐ Agree but Doesn't Apply
   - ☐ Agree and Applies
4. There is a difference between harsh criticism and honest realism in relating to your mate.
   - ☐ Disagree
   - ☐ Not Sure
   - ☐ Agree but Doesn't Apply
   - ☐ Agree and Applies
5. God honors the wife who honors her husband.
   - ☐ Disagree
   - ☐ Not Sure
   - ☐ Agree but Doesn't Apply
   - ☐ Agree and Applies

Now sit down with your mate—or if you're unmarried, with a close friend—and discuss the "why" behind your answers.

Chapter 4

ABSALOM: THE REBEL PRINCE CHARMING

2 Samuel 13–18

From "Dallas" to "Dynasty," soap operas are seething caldrons of power, greed, lust, adultery, intrigue, and treachery. Nothing is sacred; no one is safe. Everything and everyone is up for grabs. It's survival of the fittest, on both a personal and a corporate level. It's a dog-eat-dog world, and the puppies don't make it. In these jungles of tangled family relationships, brother is pitted against brother, wife against husband, father against son. Such is the stuff that television melodrama is made of.

But scripts like these are not the inventions of imaginative writers fertile with fantasy; they originate in real life, with real people. One such family feud is found in 2 Samuel, where a son's imprisoned bitterness toward his father breaks its fetters, allowing rebellion and revenge to run loose, unrestrained. And since this was the king's son, not only was the king endangered but also the kingdom itself.

This royal family lived in a fishbowl, and their drama became nightly viewing for the entire nation. Sex, murder, cover-ups, ambitions, political intrigue, power struggles—they had enough plots, subplots, and counterplots to fill seasons of programming on every major network. Were it a television drama, the family's story might be titled simply "Israel" or "Kingdom," for the story is centered on David, the greatest king in Israel's history. Of course, the advertising hype boasts a cast of thousands, but for this episode, the main stars—listed in alphabetical order—are Absalom and David.

Absalom's Home

David's immediate family tree, from which sprouted the rotten fruit of Absalom, resembles an overgrown peach orchard: seven wives in Hebron and an unnumbered amount of wives and concubines in Jerusalem. With his wives alone, David fathered twenty sons and one daughter.[1] With boughs weighed down so heavily, it

---

1. See 2 Samuel 3:2–5, 13–14; 5:14–16; 1 Chronicles 3:5–9; 2 Chronicles 11:18.

is no wonder that some of the offspring would fall from the tree to rot underneath its very branches.

Such was the case with Absalom. But the finger of blame cannot be pointed solely at the young rebel. Because of his father's polygamy, Absalom grew up in a fragmented home. Also, Absalom saw within his home some incomprehensible inconsistencies in David's life.

However, the passing of years covers a multitude of sins for history's heroes. Now we look upon David with awe and admiration. The headlines we remember are: "Shepherd Boy Slays Giant" . . . "War Hero Becomes King" . . . "David: A Man after God's Own Heart." On every street corner, newsboys called out "Read all about it!" and boasted their king's exploits.

At home, however, Absalom got the inside scoop on his father's life. Absalom's family was fraught with rivalry and rife with court gossip during Absalom's formative years. Old enough to understand, Absalom witnessed his father's involvement with Bathsheba and the ensuing cover-up, which made Watergate look like a child's game of hide-and-seek.[2]

The unveiling of hypocrisy before a child's eyes produces deeply painful, often bitter results. It did with Absalom. May I get painfully personal with you for a moment? What story is your family reading about your life? Are they buying the journalistic hype at the news-stand, or are they doing some investigative reporting of their own behind the scenes? What, then, are they uncovering—honesty or hypocrisy?

You can expend a lot of energy—as David did—in covering up, or you can channel that energy into living your life in such a way that a cover-up isn't necessary. Remember, your life—front page, sports page, comics—is being read by impressionable eyes. Eyes that don't easily forgive or forget.

Absalom's Bitterness

Professionally, David was enmeshed in the affairs of state and diplomacy. Domestically, with all his wives, concubines, and children, what time he had at home was spread far too thin to be effective. It is no surprise, then, that in jumping from chapter 3 to chapter 13—a leap of twenty years—no mention is made of Absalom.

2. Read the inside news of David's clandestine sexual charades, the murderous cover-up, and the public scandal in 2 Samuel 11–12.

He's simply overlooked by the biblical writer, which undoubtedly was what happened in his relationship with David. He was simply *overlooked* by a father who was either too busy or too tired for too long.

It is easy to overlook little things, especially when it comes to your children. Too tired to play ball when you get home from work, you overlook the fact that your child has waited all day—which for a child seems an eternity—for you to come home. Too busy with work taken home from the office or with domestic chores, you overlook reading the bedtime story or tucking the children into bed. Too enmeshed in the newspaper or your favorite TV program, you overlook the fact that your child is struggling with a confusing homework assignment and could really use your help.

Little things, overlooked. In his *Poor Richard's Almanac*, Benjamin Franklin shows the importance of little things and how disastrous it can be when they are overlooked.

> For want of a nail the shoe was lost; for want of a shoe the horse was lost; and for want of a horse the rider was lost; being overtaken and slain by the enemy, all for want of care about a horseshoe nail.[3]

Amnon's Violation of Tamar

An incident that further deepened Absalom's bitterness toward his father is described in chapter 13. David's oldest son, Amnon, had fallen in love with his half sister, Tamar, who was Absalom's sister. Through subterfuge Amnon was able to get the girl alone, then he raped her (vv. 1–14).

After his sexual appetite was sated, Amnon's feelings toward Tamar changed. We read that "the hatred with which he hated her was greater than the love with which he had loved her" (v. 15). Tamar fled, hurt and humiliated, to stay with Absalom (v. 20).

King David heard of Amnon's crime and became "very angry" (v. 21), but there is no record of any reprimand.[4] It was an unpleasant incident and David wanted it kept out of the papers, so he swept the dirt under the family rug. Undoubtedly, this failure to act further fueled the fires of Absalom's burning hatred toward his dad.

---

3. Benjamin Franklin in *Five Thousand Quotations for All Occasions*, ed. Lewis C. Henry (Garden City, N.Y.: Doubleday and Co., 1945), p. 28.

4. The Mosaic Law clearly states that such an offense is an abomination and that the offender should be disciplined by being cut off from the nation (Lev. 18).

Absalom's Revenge against Amnon

After two years of letting his revenge simmer on the back burner, Absalom turns up the heat in a plot to murder Amnon. With David's approval, Absalom arranges for Amnon to take the grand tour of his sheepshearing enterprise in Baal-hazor. However, under this facade of friendliness, Absalom brews a covert plot that he delegates to his servants: "See now, when Amnon's heart is merry with wine, and when I say to you, 'Strike Amnon,' then put him to death. Do not fear; have not I myself commanded you? Be courageous and be valiant" (v. 28). With the plot unfolding like the structured scenes of a Hollywood murder mystery, Amnon is killed, and Absalom flees for three years to hide with his grandfather, Talmai, king of Geshur. Eventually, Absalom is recalled to Jerusalem and resettled, but he is not reconciled to his father (14:1–24).

Absalom's Popularity

Verses 25–26 give us a glimpse of Absalom's physical appearance and popularity.

> Now in all Israel was no one as handsome as Absalom, so highly praised; from the sole of his foot to the crown of his head there was no defect in him. And when he cut the hair of his head (and it was at the end of every year that he cut it, for it was heavy on him so he cut it), he weighed the hair of his head at 200 shekels by the king's weight.

Absalom's Conspiracy

The motive and method of Absalom's conspiracy against David bubbles to the surface during the two years he resides, estranged from his father, in Jerusalem.

Absalom's Motive

For two years, Absalom has been allowed to live in Jerusalem but not permitted to see his father (vv. 21–24). In a play-me-or-trade-me gesture, Absalom forces Joab, one of David's men, to negotiate a meeting with him and his father: "Now therefore, let me see the king's face; and if there is iniquity in me, let him put me to death" (v. 32b).

A meeting is arranged in which Absalom prostrates himself before the king, and then the king kisses him. The scene has all the external staging of a reconciliation, but something is missing. Both men seem to be playing out contrived roles—acting out parts—rather than reacting with genuine emotion. Undoubtedly, Absalom no longer looks to David as a father with whom to be reconciled, but as a foe to be reckoned with.

Absalom's Method

With his personal charm and political charisma (14:25; 15:1–5), "Absalom stole away the hearts of the men of Israel" (v. 6). Cunningly, he uses his influence to construct his own cabinet with men who had defected from David's circle of leadership (v. 12). The ground-swell conspiracy rippled through the palace right under David's nose.

Suddenly caught in the vortex of a *coup d'état*, David and his servants flee the palace (vv. 13–14). As a personal affront to his father, Absalom went in to the royal harem, whom David had left behind, and had sex with them on the same porch where David had had relations with Bathsheba (16:20–23).

Absalom's Death

As David organized an army to recapture Jerusalem, he ordered his men to deal gently with Absalom. Meanwhile, Absalom, riding under an overgrown oak tree, got his long hair entangled in its branches and was left hanging helplessly in midair. Finding Absalom in the tree, Joab drove three spears into his heart.

In spite of the fact that this proverbial burr in David's saddle had been removed, wounds of regret remained, goading his conscience. Hearing the news of Absalom's death, David responds with the greatest remorse.

> And the king was deeply moved and went up to the chamber over the gate and wept. And thus he said as he walked, "O my son Absalom, my son, my son Absalom! Would I had died instead of you, O Absalom, my son, my son!" (18:33)

Some Concluding Applications

The story of Absalom's relationship with his father is a tragic one, but we can learn some valuable lessons through their painful mistakes.

First: *An unhappy home breeds unbalanced children.* It does bear true that we reap what we sow. Where wheat isn't planted, tares of indulgence grow in its place, making for a backbreaking harvest. Are you cultivating a happy home, or are you too tired or too busy to sow the right kind of seed (see Prov. 24:30–34)? Remember, if you sow nothing, you can expect to reap only weeds.

Second: *An undisciplined family breeds insecurity and resentment.* We have no record of David ever disciplining his children for their many wrongs. Children need enforced boundaries to give them a sense of security. They need a degree of freedom, but only within the secure grounds provided by well-constructed fences. When children cut holes in the fences you have erected, and you fail to hold them accountable by bringing them back and mending the fences, they question your love for them (see Prov. 13:24). Eventually, this leads to resentment and, ultimately, to rebellion.

Third: *An unreconciled relationship breeds sores that never heal.* Even the death of the resented person can't stanch ill feelings. Unreconciled hurt has a way of reaching out from the grave and wagging its bony finger at the one still living.

Forgiveness is the only way to restore estranged relationships— not geographical separation or even death. Paul's advice here is timely.

> Let all bitterness and wrath and anger and clamor and slander be put away from you, along with all malice. And be kind to one another, tender-hearted, forgiving each other, just as God in Christ also has forgiven you. (Eph. 4:31–32)

 ## Living Insights STUDY ONE

The old saying goes, Like father, like son. Does Absalom remind you of his dad? Let's walk through some territory in 2 Samuel with the express purpose of comparing and contrasting.

As you read 2 Samuel 3 and 13–18, jot down first the characteristics seen in both men. Then write down the characteristics that contrast David and Absalom.

Characteristics of David and Absalom

Similar Traits: _____

_____

_____

_____

_____

Contrasting Traits: _____

_____

_____

_____

🍇 *Living Insights* STUDY TWO

Some very timely and practical lessons emerge from this study of family relationships. Let's spend time on each one. You may want to do this together as a family, in a study group, or alone. We're personalizing here . . . jumping right out of the study guide into *your* life.

- *An unhappy home breeds unbalanced children.* Do you agree?

_____

Can you think of illustrations you've observed?

_____

What are some definite ways you can contribute to making your home happy? Name a few.

_____

_____

_____

- *An undisciplined family breeds insecurity and resentment.* What priority do luxury and leisure have in your home?

_____

_____

How is discipline handled in your home?

_____

_____

If you had to pinpoint a weak area in your discipline, what
would it be?

_____

_____

During this next week, how can you work on that weakness?

_____

_____

_____

• *An unreconciled relationship breeds sores that never heal.* How
would you rate your family relationships?

_____

_____

_____

Have they been suffering due to "busyness"?

_____

_____

List three ways you can resolve this problem right away, then
close by asking God for strength to follow through on your plans.

1. _____

2. _____

3. _____

Chapter 5

REHOBOAM:
THE RECKLESS PHONY

1 Kings 11–14

With a dazzling array of movie stars, expensive sets, and special effects, the movie industry makes its living by manufacturing illusions—making something phony look real. The words *lights . . . camera . . . action* introduce us to an artificial world constructed from scripts, actors, rehearsals, veneered sets, and special lighting. It's all contrived to create a sense of reality.

But true reality does not end up on the reels of 35-mm film to be shown in the theater. True reality takes place off camera, behind the scenes.

For example, the 1939 classic film *The Wizard of Oz* created a host of illusions that simulated reality: the tornado that threatened Dorothy's farm . . . the uprooting of the farmhouse into the vortex of the tornado . . . the Wicked Witch's army of winged monkeys flying through the air. From our point of view these all seem real, but from the other side of the camera we get a picture of the behind-the-scenes reality.

The tornado was created by attaching a huge muslin sock to a movable steel structure at the top, and at the bottom to a small car that would zigzag back and forth to pull the tip of the huge sock through a slot in the stage floor. To heighten the illusion, fuller's earth and compressed air were fed into the sock from the bottom with air hoses. The porous muslin let enough of the fuller's earth through to create a cloud of dust that disguised the sock.

The model of the farmhouse used in the tornado sequence was just three feet tall. First, the house was photographed falling on a floor painted to look like the sky. Then, to create the illusion that the tornado was picking up the house, the film was run backward.

And the threatening army of monkeys? Most were an intimidating six inches high, cast in rubber, and hung by piano wire one-thousandth of an inch thick. There were only about a dozen real people dressed in monkey costumes, suspended on somewhat thicker wire. Underneath their monkey suits were small battery-driven electric motors adapted from windshield wiper motors that made the wings go up and down.[1]

Sitting in a darkened theater and seeing the moviemaker's finished product, it's difficult to spot the socks and piano wires of special effects. However, when we go behind the scenes—off camera—it's easy to spot what's phony and what's real. In this study, we're going to take a tour of the back lots of a man named Rehoboam, to see what's for real and what's phony about his life.

The Roots of Rehoboam's Phoniness

You don't have to trace Rehoboam's genealogical roots very far to find the source of his on-camera, off-camera, duplicitous life. Rehoboam's father was Solomon, and his mother was Naamah, a distinguished Ammonite woman.[2] Undoubtedly, Rehoboam had read his father's Song of Songs, which extolled the sanctity and beauty of the marriage relationship.

However, Solomon's seven hundred wives and three hundred concubines surely revealed a discrepancy between what he published and what went on in his private life (1 Kings 11:3). In order to make his royal marriages effective, Solomon thought it necessary to build temples for the more important wives living with him in Jerusalem (vv. 5–8). International marriages commonly required the recognition of foreign deities, and Solomon's were no exception. As a result, these wives "turned his heart away after other gods" (v. 4). Again, Rehoboam saw in his father a dual standard: confessing one God, yet tolerating the influential presence of many foreign gods.

Finally, raised on his father's Proverbs—which stressed wisdom and self-discipline—Rehoboam saw Solomon living out the experiences of a self-indulgent fool as recorded, autobiographically, in Ecclesiastes. When Solomon died, Rehoboam succeeded him at the age of forty-one (v. 43). His first decision as head of state revealed his two-sided character.

1. Taken from *The Making of the Wizard of Oz*, by Aljean Harmetz (New York, N.Y.: Alfred A. Knopf, 1981).

2. The Ammonites were descendants of Lot's youngest daughter. She lived in Sodom, where all the sensual cults of illicit sex, along with the pagan gods Molech and Milcom, had their roots. Worship of these deities involved sacrificing children in a furnace of fire. "Excavations in Palestine have uncovered piles of ashes and remains of infant skeletons in cemeteries around heathen altars, pointing to the widespread practice of this cruel abomination." Merrill F. Unger, *Archaeology and the Old Testament* (Grand Rapids, Mich.: Zondervan Publishing House, 1970), p. 279.

The Examples of Rehoboam's Phoniness

Four incidents in Rehoboam's reign serve to strip the veneer of righteousness that overlaid his life and reveal the cheap, splintered plywood of wickedness. For forty-one years Rehoboam had lived in his father's shadow, where he learned to play a rehearsed role for the public eye, all the while nurturing—behind the scenes, away from the camera—a life of self-indulgence and expediency.

The Incident regarding Taxation

Upon Rehoboam's taking the throne, the people came to him with a request.

> "Your father made our yoke hard; therefore lighten the hard service of your father and his heavy yoke which he put on us, and we will serve you." (12:4)

Rehoboam sent them away for three days in order to take the matter under advisement.

> And King Rehoboam consulted with the elders who had served his father Solomon while he was still alive, saying, "How do you counsel me to answer this people?" Then they spoke to him, saying, "If you will be a servant to this people today, will serve them, grant them their petition, and speak good words to them, then they will be your servants forever." (vv. 6–7)

Although Rehoboam went through the motions of seeking counsel from his father's veteran advisers, he rejected their advice and turned to his peers.

> So he said to them, "What counsel do you give that we may answer this people who have spoken to me, saying, 'Lighten the yoke which your father put on us'?" And the young men who grew up with him spoke to him, saying, "Thus you shall say to this people who spoke to you, saying, 'Your father made our yoke heavy, now you make it lighter for us!' But you shall speak to them, 'My little finger is thicker than my father's loins! Whereas my father loaded you with a heavy yoke, I will add to your yoke; my

father disciplined you with whips, but I will discipline you with scorpions.' " (vv. 9–11)[3]

Verse 15 states that "the king did not listen to the people." Deep down inside, Rehoboam had no intention of giving ear to the needs of the people. As a result, civil war ensued (vv. 16–24). The ten tribes of the north revolted and established a separate nation under the name Israel, making Jeroboam their leader. Rehoboam was left with only two tribes, Judah and Benjamin, forming the nation of Judah.

The Incident regarding Civil War

Through a man named Shemaiah, God told Rehoboam not to fight against his relatives in the northern kingdom.

> "Thus says the Lord, 'You shall not go up or fight against your relatives; return every man to his house, for this thing is from Me.' " So they listened to the words of the Lord and returned from going against Jeroboam. (2 Chron. 11:4)

On camera, Rehoboam appears obedient. But off camera, he actually beefs up his country's defenses for war.

> Rehoboam lived in Jerusalem and built cities for defense in Judah. Thus he built Bethlehem, Etam, Tekoa, Beth-zur, Soco, Adullam, Gath, Mareshah, Ziph, Adoraim, Lachish, Azekah, Zorah, Aijalon, and Hebron, which are fortified cities in Judah and in Benjamin. He also strengthened the fortresses and put officers in them and stores of food, oil and wine. And he put shields and spears in every city and strengthened them greatly. So he held Judah and Benjamin. (vv. 5–12)

Hardly the picture of someone relaxing and trusting God!

The Incident regarding the Capital City

On the surface, Jerusalem looked as if it were the city of the Lord. In reality, it had become the city of Naamah, Rehoboam's Ammonite mother.

---

3. The scorpion referred to here was a lash that had a single handle but nine to twelve leather straps embedded with pieces of bone or metal. The whip was only a wooden handle with a single leather strap.

> Now Rehoboam the son of Solomon reigned in Judah. Rehoboam was forty-one years old when he became king, and he reigned seventeen years in Jerusalem, the city which the Lord had chosen from all the tribes of Israel to put His name there. And his mother's name was Naamah the Ammonitess. And Judah did evil in the sight of the Lord, and they provoked Him to jealousy more than all that their fathers had done, with the sins which they committed. For they also built for themselves high places and sacred pillars and Asherim on every high hill and beneath every luxuriant tree. And there were also male cult prostitutes in the land. They did according to all the abominations of the nations which the Lord dispossessed before the sons of Israel. (1 Kings 14:21–24)

When Solomon brought his pagan wives into the city, he erected altars and effigies to their gods. Apparently, Naamah's influence exceeded that of his other wives. The sensuality and human sacrifice that accompanied her form of worship brought abominable conditions to Jerusalem. On the surface, Jerusalem bore the Lord's name. It was His city. However, the city, like Rehoboam, was really a whitewashed tomb, full of death and decay.

The Incident regarding Solomon's Shields

Because of Rehoboam's unfaithfulness to Him, God led the king of Egypt, Shishak, against Jerusalem. This resulted in the pillage of both the Lord's house and the king's palace. Following the plunder, Rehoboam's character again shows through his shallow facade.

> So Shishak king of Egypt came up against Jerusalem, and took the treasures of the house of the Lord and the treasures of the king's palace. He took everything; he even took the golden shields which Solomon had made. Then King Rehoboam made shields of bronze in their place, and committed them to the care of the commanders of the guard who guarded the door of the king's house. And it happened as often as the king entered the house of the Lord, the guards came and carried them and then brought them back into the guards' room. (2 Chron. 12:9–11)

First Kings 10 catalogs the vast array of opulent wealth that Solomon had in his palace. Regarding the shields, he had made "200 large shields of beaten gold, using 600 shekels of gold on each large shield. And he made 300 shields of beaten gold, using three minas of gold on each shield" (vv. 16–17a).

In hopes that the public wouldn't discover the theft, Rehoboam cleverly arranged for shields made out of bronze to replace the gold ones. He worked surreptitiously behind the scenes to cover up the loss, and through his special effects department, managed to make the phony bronze substitutes seem like the real thing. To strengthen the illusion, he kept the shields from close public view. Another example of his hypocrisy and phoniness.

A Brief Summary

In conclusion, we see four areas of hypocrisy in Rehoboam's life. He said he sought counsel, but he never really listened to the people. He said he would not fight, but behind the scenes he was fortifying his cities for battle. He lived in a city that was to have the name of the Lord, but it actually had the name of his mother, Naamah, a worshiper of pagan gods. Finally, he sought to cover up the loss of the stolen gold shields by replacing them with stand-ins made of bronze. In these four scenes we see Rehoboam as a consummate actor skilled at performances aimed to please the public eye.

Personal Application

The word *hypocrite* comes from the Greek word *hupokritēs*, which is an old word for "actor" that described a character on the ancient Greek stage who wore a mask as he recited his lines. It's easy to live a theatrical, on-camera existence, like Rehoboam, aimed at pleasing the public, while our off-camera, behind-the-scenes life is full of self-indulgence and deception. But though we may fool the audience, we will never fool the Lord. He will always be the Critic who sees behind our masks and into our hearts.

> "Woe to you, scribes and Pharisees, hypocrites! For you are like whitewashed tombs which on the outside appear beautiful, but inside they are full of dead men's bones and all uncleanness. Even so you too outwardly appear righteous to men, but inwardly you are full of hypocrisy and lawlessness." (Matt. 23:27–28)

If you're living an on-stage, off-stage double life, remember that in the balcony sits a Critic whose Word cuts through the fluff of your pretended role and pierces "as far as the division of soul and spirit, of both joints and marrow, and [is] able to judge the thoughts and intentions of the heart. And there is no creature hidden from His sight, but all things are open and laid bare to [His] eyes" (Heb. 4:12–13).

 Living Insights

Rehoboam had the outward appearance of having it all together. But a closer look reveals that inside it was all falling apart. Let's take a closer look at this man's life.

Take some time to read 1 Kings 11–14. Get a perspective on Rehoboam's life and reign, and try to put his life into a detailed outline. Follow it through to his death in 14:31. After you've completed the outline, put a check by everything in the outline that was fake, phony—surface stuff.

_____

_____

_____

_____

_____

_____

_____

_____

_____

_____

Does anything you've found hit home in your life? Talk with God about this study.

It's one thing to *read* about a phony. It's quite another thing to *be* one. Have you given it much thought recently? Let's do that.

Do you have a public life and a private life? How different are they? Using the following chart, see what you can learn about yourself. Circle a specific area you can work on this week. Complete this chart slowly and thoughtfully.

What Others See	What God Sees

Chapter 6

NAAMAN AND GEHAZI: CHARACTERS IN CONTRAST

2 Kings 5

*P*oetic justice is a literary term first introduced in England by Thomas Rymer in 1678. It denotes that the characters in a drama essentially reap the harvest of what they sow—for the virtuous, reward; for the wicked, punishment. It can be easily seen in Nahum Tate's 1681 revision of Shakespeare's most pessimistic work, *King Lear.* In his revision, Tate deletes the character of the Fool and adds a happy ending. The villains die and the heroes live. Lear is restored to his throne, and Cordelia weds Edgar.

In 2 Kings 5, a similar type of drama is enacted that forever changes the course of two men's lives. The men: Naaman and Gehazi. The first was a leper; the second, a servant of God's prophet Elisha. In an example of poetic justice, a surprising change takes place in the lives of both men. The leper becomes a servant of God; the servant, in turn, becomes a leper.

As the curtain rises on this drama, we'll be able to see Naaman and Gehazi with front-row clarity. And all the character lines etching their faces will be revealed as the footlights of God's Word wash over them. We'll see that both faces are lined and shadowed with unbelief, which in Naaman manifests itself as pride and in Gehazi as greed.

Naaman

Descriptions of Naaman

In the opening credits, Naaman is described in glowing terms.

> Now Naaman, captain of the army of the king of Aram, was a great man with his master, and highly respected, because by him the Lord had given victory to Aram. The man was also a valiant warrior, but he was a leper.[1] (2 Kings 5:1)

---

1. Leprosy is "a slowly progressing and intractable disease characterized by subcutaneous nodules . . . , scabs or cuticular crusts . . . and white shining spots appearing to be deeper

Naaman was a high-ranking officer in the Syrian army. His war record was impressive: he was instrumental in bringing peace to the land. His personal references were impeccable: "a great man with his master, and highly respected." And, not only was he a great military leader, he was also a "valiant warrior"—something like a highly respected player-coach. However, one physical flaw dogged Naaman's every footstep: *he was a leper.*

Leprosy, in biblical times, was a dreaded skin disease. Those who had it—at least in Israel—were outcasts of society. They were often banished to live in isolated colonies, ostracized by the community (see Lev. 13, especially vv. 45–46). Although Syrian social regulations were not as stringent as Israel's, the diseased skin of a leper was a stigma that shadowed the person all through life. It was a disease that could be pronounced cleansed by the priest but could not be cured (Lev. 14).

Events Leading to Naaman's Cure

Even before Naaman's conversion, God was at work coupling a chain of events that would lead to the cure of his leprosy, "because by him the Lord had given victory" (v. 1). Coming to verse 2, we see a small but indispensable link in that chain.

> Now the Arameans had gone out in bands, and had taken captive a little girl from the land of Israel; and she waited on Naaman's wife. And she said to her mistress, "I wish that my master were with the prophet who is in Samaria! Then he would cure him of his leprosy." (2 Kings 5:2–3)

A "little girl," yet mightily used by God to set Naaman on a life-changing course to leprosy's cure. The next link in God's chain of events is a bigger one—Naaman's master, the king of Aram.

> And Naaman went in and told his master, saying, "Thus and thus spoke the girl who is from the land of Israel." Then the king of Aram said, "Go now, and I will send a letter to the king of Israel." And

---

than the skin. . . . The disease is a zymotic affection produced by a microbe discovered by Hansen in 1871. It is contagious, although not very readily communicated by casual contact. . . . [In] those forms in which nodular growths are the most prominent features . . . the limbs often drop off." *The International Standard Bible Encyclopaedia*, gen. ed. James Orr (Grand Rapids, Mich.: William B. Eerdmans Publishing Co., 1976), vol. 3, p. 1867.

he departed and took with him ten talents of silver and six thousand shekels of gold and ten changes of clothes. (vv. 4–5)

Notice Naaman's thinking as an unbeliever. The first thing that comes to his mind is, "I'll give money. I'll buy my cure." So, with Gucci bags full of gold, garment bags stuffed with a valuable collection of designer clothes, and a letter of entrée, he sets off with the wind of optimism in his sails.

And he brought the letter to the king of Israel, saying, "And now as this letter comes to you, behold, I have sent Naaman my servant to you, that you may cure him of his leprosy." And it came about when the king of Israel read the letter, that he tore his clothes and said, "Am I God, to kill and to make alive, that this man is sending word to me to cure a man of his leprosy? But consider now, and see how he is seeking a quarrel against me." (vv. 6–7)

The request literally tears the king of Israel to pieces with its superhuman demands. He replies, exasperated: "Am I God . . . ?" Upon reflection, the king imagines that the request might be some ploy to create an incident between the two kingdoms. Fortunately for the king, the matter reaches Elisha's ears and is immediately delegated to him.

And it happened when Elisha the man of God heard that the king of Israel had torn his clothes, that he sent word to the king, saying, "Why have you torn your clothes? Now let him come to me, and he shall know that there is a prophet in Israel." (v. 8)

Naaman wastes no time beating a direct path to the prophet's door.

So Naaman came with his horses and his chariots, and stood at the doorway of the house of Elisha. And Elisha sent a messenger to him, saying, "Go and wash in the Jordan seven times, and your flesh shall be restored to you and you shall be clean." (vv. 9–10)[2]

2. Elisha's prescription is reminiscent of Leviticus 14:1–8, yet without all the trappings of ceremonial detail.

Once the entourage reaches Elisha's house, Naaman is greeted in a manner that seems to him totally inhospitable and humiliating. First, he is not invited in but is left to stand in Elisha's doorway. Second, Elisha doesn't come to greet him but only sends his messenger. Third, the prescription the messenger brings hardly fills the bill of what Naaman had expected from so great a prophet as Elisha. For a man who had been accustomed to buying everything he wanted, the prescription was a hard pill to swallow.

Try to envision the emotional backdrop. Here is a man more used to giving orders than taking them, more used to paying his own way than receiving gifts. Here is a man who had traveled a long way and had just come from an emotionally wrenching reception with Israel's king. He had just ridden nonstop to the probably remote, out-of-the-way home of some foreign religious fanatic. But to his chagrin, he is greeted with humiliation instead of hospitality.

Standing at the doorway with his entourage looking on, he reads this little crumpled-up note given him by Elisha's servant. And, as if it weren't bad enough for a Syrian to come to a Jew's land, he was expected to do some silly, ritual dip in the muddy Jordan river. Understanding the background and Naaman's pride, his reply is predictable.

> But Naaman was furious and went away and said, "Behold, I thought, 'He will surely come out to me, and stand and call on the name of the Lord his God, and wave his hand over the place, and cure the leper.' Are not Abanah and Pharpar, the rivers of Damascus, better than all the waters of Israel? Could I not wash in them and be clean?" So he turned and went away in a rage. (vv. 11–12)

Then, just as Naaman threatened to break the chain, another minor link holds the events leading to his cure in place.

> Then his servants came near and spoke to him and said, "My father, had the prophet told you to do some great thing, would you not have done it? How much more then, when he says to you, 'Wash, and be clean'?" (v. 13)

In spite of his rage, Naaman realizes that the servant's reasoning is right and reacts more rationally.

> So he went down and dipped himself seven times in the Jordan, according to the word of the man of

God; and his flesh was restored like the flesh of a little child, and he was clean. (v. 14)

An Observation about Naaman

In Naaman's defense, we can't overlook the fact that he listened to the advice of those under him—the little servant girl (vv. 2–3), Elisha's servant (v. 10), his own servants (v. 13). God sometimes works in strange ways to bring about His will. He speaks through His Word (Heb. 4:12), but He also speaks through the whirlwind (Job 38:1). He speaks through the prophets (Heb. 1:1), but He also speaks through Balaam's donkey (Num. 22:28).

It appears, then, that the only way to hear all that God has to say to us is to develop a listening ear and a learning heart. Proverbs instructs us that "in abundance of counselors there is victory" (11:14b). Like some of the Old Testament prophets, those counselors can occasionally come in strange garb—a sunset . . . a psalm . . . a sparrow . . . even a servant.

How are your ears? Have you been in for a hearing test lately— or should I say a *listening* test? Try listening to and learning from a little child—as Naaman did. If you can pass this test, God is beginning to train your ears to hear His footsteps . . . soft but certain amid the traffic of everyday life.

Gehazi

Verses 15–19 form a literary bridge by which Naaman and Gehazi are brought together. Elated with his cleansing, Naaman rushes to thank Elisha and makes a genuine profession of faith: "Behold now, I know that there is no God in all the earth, but in Israel" (v. 15). Then, he not only urges Elisha to accept a present of gratitude but upon Elisha's refusal, he urges him again. Meanwhile, standing in the shadows, Elisha's servant Gehazi overhears this volley of offers and refusals. You can almost hear the dollar signs ringing in his head as he tabulates the profit.

> But Gehazi, the servant of Elisha the man of God, thought, "Behold, my master has spared this Naaman the Aramean, by not receiving from his hands what he brought. As the Lord lives, I will run after him and take something from him." (v. 20)

Seizing an opportunity for financial gain, Gehazi slips out the back to catch up to Naaman.

So Gehazi pursued Naaman. When Naaman saw one running after him, he came down from the chariot to meet him and said, "Is all well?" (v. 21)

It is at this point that Gehazi's imagination sprouts full blooms of colorful lies.

And he said, "All is well. My master has sent me, saying, 'Behold, just now two young men of the sons of the prophets have come to me from the hill country of Ephraim. Please give them a talent of silver and two changes of clothes.'" And Naaman said, "Be pleased to take two talents." And he urged him, and bound two talents of silver in two bags with two changes of clothes, and gave them to two of his servants; and they carried them before him. (vv. 22–23)

First lie: "My master has sent me." *Second lie:* "Two young men of the sons of the prophets have come" to stay, and money is needed for their lodging. *Third lie:* "My master has sent me, *saying*" (emphasis added). He attributes this third lie to Elisha's lips. Gehazi returns to Elisha's house, where he covertly stashes the coins. Although not caught with his hands in the cookie jar, Gehazi has crumbs all over his red face.

When he came to the hill, he took them from their hand and deposited them in the house, and he sent the men away, and they departed. But he went in and stood before his master. And Elisha said to him, "Where have you been, Gehazi?" And he said, "Your servant went nowhere." (vv. 24–25)

Fourth lie: "Your servant went nowhere."

We are often advised never to say never. But one *never* that seems appropriate is to never, never lie to a *prophet*. Of all the people in the world most likely to see through the scam and into the heart of things, it's a prophet! Listen to the penetrating questions that pierce through Gehazi's flimsy lies. Then hear the scathing indictment.

Then he said to him, "Did not my heart go with you, when the man turned from his chariot to meet you? Is it a time to receive money and to receive clothes and olive groves and vineyards and sheep and oxen and male and female servants? Therefore, the leprosy of Naaman shall cleave to you and to your descendants forever." So he went out from his presence a leper as white as snow. (vv. 26–27)

An Ironic Ending

Irony is a literary term that refers to a situation which is the tragic reverse of what is expected. Thus, it is ironic that King Arthur's Round Table was destroyed by Lancelot—the very man who helped build it. It is ironic that Eve expected great happiness by eating the forbidden fruit when, in fact, it brought her great sorrow.

And it is ironic that Naaman, the Syrian, came away from Elisha *cleansed* while Gehazi, the Jew who lived as a servant in Elisha's own house, came away *cursed* (see Luke 4:27). It is ironic, too, that Naaman, the leper (2 Kings 5:1), became the servant (v. 18), and Gehazi, the servant (v. 20), became the leper (v. 27). In a downpour of poetic justice, Naaman's loose change became Gehazi's leprous curse. The truth about Gehazi leaked through his roof of thatched lies to expose his greed and drench it in God's sudden and torrential judgment.[3]

If your life were made into a play, would the main character's flaws be visible—like Naaman's leprosy—or would they be hidden —like Gehazi's greed? Would the main character listen to the advice of servants—like Naaman—or would he be evasive to the words of his master—like Gehazi? Has your main character made a public profession of faith—like Naaman's washing in the Jordan—or is there a private world of hidden sin thatched with lies?

These are questions you need to come to grips with—if you want your life to have a happy ending instead of a tragic one.

 Living Insights _____ STUDY ONE

It would be so easy if, as in the old western movies, the good guys all wore white hats and the bad guys all wore black ones. But life is not usually so neat and tidy. The truth is, everyone is a little bit of a hero—and a little bit of a villain.

Read through 2 Kings 5 and summarize which characteristics you share with our hero Naaman and with the villianous Gehazi.

---

3. Swift and certain judgment functions as a deterrent against evil (see Eccles. 8:11).

Characteristics I Share with:

Verse	Naaman

Verse	Gehazi

What could you do to be a little less like Gehazi and a little more like Naaman?

_____

_____

_____

_____

_____

_____

Living Insights

Are you, like Gehazi, guilty of deception? This is such a serious matter—please deal with it before the roof comes crashing down around you. It's so vital to clear your conscience before God and, perhaps also, before the ones you've been deceiving: Dad, Mom, sons, daughters, employers, employees, neighbors, church friends . . . whomever. On a separate sheet, write out a confession to the person you've deceived. Then, when you've finished, determine to call, write, or make contact in person and clear the air of the deception.

Chapter 7

JABEZ: DISABLED
BUT NOT DISQUALIFIED

1 Chronicles 4:9–10

Thousands of the world's best athletes compete in the Olympic Games. Each Olympian's body has been carefully sculpted, fine-tuned to guarantee optimum performance in the individual's event.

Marathoners—slight, twiglike—must be able to endure a rapid pulse rate for more than twenty-six miles, so they spend their training time toning and expanding the heart.

The swimmer's body—with its sturdy trunk—must be prepared to propel itself through the water, powerfully, forcefully, like a well-oiled machine.

And the gymnasts—limber, catlike—must be swift enough to catch bars with their thighs . . . to complete the 2½ flip with a twist before reaching the floor.

Every Olympian has what it takes to win. All are at their best, bearing no disabilities. But this is not the case in the game of life.

The Old Testament gives us a prime example in Jabez, who was disabled but refused to let his handicap hamper his performance. He is an unknown competitor who appears on the scriptural playing field briefly and goes for the gold, never to be mentioned again. Jabez may not have made the "Hall of Faith" in Hebrews 11. His name may not even appear on a single game card in Bible Trivia. But his example—one of faith and fortitude—is challenging. His attitude, revolutionary.

A Glance at Jabez

If you blink, you'll miss it. But rising out of the dust of 1 Chronicles is a two-verse oasis where you catch a brief glimpse of a man who will whet your thirst for God.

> And Jabez was more honorable than his brothers, and his mother named him Jabez saying, "Because I bore him with pain." Now Jabez called on the God of Israel, saying, "Oh that Thou wouldst bless me indeed, and enlarge my border, and that Thy hand

might be with me, and that Thou wouldst keep me from harm, that it may not pain me!" And God granted him what he requested.

His Name

His mother named him Jabez, which means "pain," "distress," or "vexation." The verse tells us that his mother "bore him with pain." This does not mean that she named him "pain" because she had a difficult delivery, but rather that his name reveals the times of hardship into which he was born. In other words, Jabez's family viewed him as salt in the open wounds of the days they lived in. We can't be certain what kind of hardship or difficulty Jabez was born into. But we do know that he wore the tag "pain" his whole life.

His Reputation

Somehow, Jabez was able to rise above his situation, and he found himself distinguished and favored among his brothers. The life of Jabez is proof that *incredible abilities often emerge from those with the least possibilities.* Jabez had to experience and endure pain before he could ultimately triumph over it. Spurgeon writes,

> It will sometimes happen that where there is the most sorrow in the antecedents, there will be the most pleasure in the sequel. As the furious storm gives place to the clear sunshine, so the night of weeping precedes the morning of joy. Sorrow the harbinger; gladness the prince it ushers in. . . . More honourable than his brethren was the child whom his mother bore with sorrow. . . . The honour [Jabez] enjoyed would not have been worth having if it had not been vigorously contested and equitably won.[1]

His Faith

From his prayer in verse 10, we discover that Jabez was a believer. It isn't actually spelled out—it doesn't have to be. Instead of *telling* us about Jabez's faith, the writer *shows* us. We read, "Now Jabez called on the God of Israel." He offered a prayer of petition to God, for his hope was in the Lord.

---

1. Charles H. Spurgeon, *The Treasury of the Bible* (Grand Rapids, Mich.: Zondervan Publishing House, 1968), vol. 2, p. 1.

This might be a good time to ask yourself a few questions. How do others perceive your faith? Do they *listen* to your faith as you chat about it, sitting on the living room couch while you sip coffee? Or do they *see* it in your life, as you work, play, worship, love? "Little children, let us not love with word or with tongue, but in deed and truth" (1 John 3:18). While He was on earth, Jesus said, "Let your light shine before men in such a way that they may see your good works, and glorify your Father who is in heaven" (Matt. 5:16). You've heard the old adage, Actions speak louder than words. The Lord agrees. He wants us to stop the faith-talking and start faith-walking.

His Prayer

In his prayer—a prayer of motivation—Jabez asks four things of God. [2]

First: *"Bless me indeed."* The last word of this prayer is the most significant. Jabez prays with God-sanctioned *vision,* asking God not merely to bless him, but to bless him *indeed.* [3] Like a true competitor, he wanted more than just to finish the race; he wanted to win. [4]

Second: *"Enlarge my border."* With God-sanctioned *ambition,* Jabez asks God for increase. He was not content with either a usual blessing or his present ministry. He refused to fill a little space; he wanted God to expand his opportunities for service.

Third: *"Thy hand might be with me."* Jabez was wise. He knew that if God enlarged his border, he would need even more to be led

---

2. One commentary gives some interesting information on the background of Jabez's prayer. "The prayer of his, . . . which, like Jacob's, is in the form of a vow (Gen. 28:20), seems to have been uttered when he was entering on an important or critical service, for the successful execution of which he placed confidence neither on his own nor his people's prowess, but looked anxiously for the aid and blessing of God." Robert Jamieson, A. R. Fausset, and David Brown, A *Commentary on the Old and New Testaments* (Grand Rapids, Mich.: William B. Eerdmans Publishing Co., 1984), vol. 1, p. 459.

3. An excellent explanation of the "indeed blessing" is found in Spurgeon's sermon on 1 Chronicles 4:9–10. "There are many varieties of blessing. Some are blessings only in name: they gratify our wishes for a moment, but permanently disappoint our expectations. They charm the eye, but pall on the taste. Others are mere temporary blessings: they perish with the using. Though for awhile they regale the senses, they cannot satisfy the higher cravings of the soul. But, 'Oh that Thou wouldst bless me indeed!' . . . Let the grace of God prompt it, let the choice of God appoint it, let the bounty of God confer it, and then the endowment shall be something godlike indeed; something worthy of the lips that pronounce the benediction, and verily to be craved by every one who seeks honor that is substantial and enduring." Spurgeon, *Treasury of the Bible,* p. 1.

4. See 1 Corinthians 9:24, where Paul encourages us to run to win the prize.

by His hand. With God-sanctioned *cooperation*, Jabez asks for God's guidance. He isn't on a power trip. He asks for big blessings and big opportunities in ministry. And he is willing to humbly place his trust in a big God.

Fourth: *"Keep me from harm, that it may not pain me!"* Finally, Jabez asks for God-sanctioned *protection*. In choosing to use the word *pain*, Jabez draws our attention to his name, which he links to his nature. He asks the Lord for protection—protection against himself and against the pattern that was so characteristic of him. It's as if Jabez is saying, "Let me not experience the grief which my name implies, and which my sins may well produce."[5] He prays that God would save him from his pessimistic past. Jabez is weary of his life of anguish. He wants a fresh start, and he knows who to go to for help.

His Answer

The best part of this glimpse of Jabez is that "God granted him what he requested."[6] Everything he asked for, he received (compare Matt. 7:7; John 15:16; James 4:2b). It's no wonder he was distinguished among his brothers.

A Glance at Ourselves

This short, crisp, historical sketch stimulates healthy self-evaluation. It raises three questions that everyone ought to answer.

First, *What is my name?* If God were to name you by your nature, what would He name you? Critical? Short-sighted? Stubborn? Or Tolerant, Prudent, or Generous?

Second, *Where am I spiritually?* Are you content to stay in your cozy, carpeted room—not wanting to get chilled by the outside air? Or are you willing to have your sphere of influence enlarged—to fill a big place for God?

Third, *What am I asking of God?* Jabez asked big things of God, and he got them. This poem by Amy Carmichael displays Jabez's Olympic attitude.

---

5. Jamieson, Fausset, and Brown, *Commentary on the Old and New Testaments*, p. 459.

6. Unger's discussion of this prayer reminds us of the example of faith we see in Jabez's life. "God heard his faithful cry and answered his prayer, furnishing the centuries with an example of the faith in God and His redemptive grace that existed in the hearts of many Judahites." Merrill F. Unger, *Unger's Commentary on the Old Testament* (Chicago, Ill.: Moody Press, 1981), vol. 1, p. 543.

From prayer that asks that I may be
Sheltered from winds that beat on Thee,
From fearing when I should aspire,
From faltering when I should climb higher,
From silken self, O captain, free
Thy soldier who would follow Thee.

From subtle love of softening things,
From easy choices, weakenings,
Not thus are spirits fortified,
Not this way went the Crucified,
From all that dims Thy Calvary,
O Lamb of God, deliver me.

Give me the love that leads the way,
The faith that nothing can dismay,
The hope no disappointments tire,
The passion that will burn like fire,
Let me not sink to be a clod:
Make me Thy fuel, Flame of God.[7]

The Last Lap

An athlete has to be in perfect shape to compete in the Olympic Games, but there are also games for those whose bodies are far from perfect—the Special Olympics.

In these games, the equipment for every event includes wheelchairs, leg braces, and catheters. Some contestants wear Nikes; some, shoes of two different sizes; others have no feet. But in the Special Olympics, all the participants have one thing in common—the courage to overcome.

Face it—in some ways, like Jabez, we were all born handicapped. The question is, will you let your disabilities disqualify you, or will you get out on the track—with your heart, your faith, and your God?

7. Amy Carmichael, "Make Me Thy Fuel" in *Toward Jerusalem* (Fort Washington, Pa.: Christian Literature Crusade, 1961; London, England: Society for Promoting Christian Knowledge, 1950), p. 94.

Look up the following verses on contentment and paraphrase each.

Phil. 4:11b _____

_____

1 Tim. 6:6–8 _____

_____

Although God wants us to be content, too often we pat our-selves on the back, thinking that because we aren't complaining about our circumstances, we've achieved contentment. Actually, we are only wearing its facade to mask our laziness. There's a difference between an attitude that says "I'm fine right where I am" and one that says "I'm happy here, but does God have something more for me to do?" The former is passivity; the latter, true contentment.

Have you settled for less than God's best in your life? Are you ignoring His tug to go somewhere, to be something—something that would challenge you? Are you shrugging it off, deluded by a sense of false contentment? If so, describe it.

_____

_____

_____

_____

What can you do to remedy the situation?

_____

_____

_____

Jabez is a striking contrast to the meaning of his name. In a sense, he overcame himself. How about you? Let's use this time for some introspection.

What name would best describe your nature? Think back on what your personality has been like during the last six months, and jot down an answer or two.

_____

_____

Let's expand this theme. Sum up what has characterized your life during the last six months. What has been your major weakness?

_____

_____

_____

What are you going to do about this weakness? Write down your specific goals for overcoming it.

_____

_____

_____

How can you pursue God's will in this situation?

_____

_____

_____

Close with prayer, asking God for big things . . . expectantly.

Chapter 8

UZZIAH: THE KING WHO BECAME A LEPER

2 Chronicles 26

Tombstones—granite tongues of ashen gray—stand row after row in cemeteries like soldiers at attention. Epitaphs—chiseled testimonies of summarized lives—mutely face the sun . . . the rain . . . the wind . . . the snow, calling out to the generations that remain. Epitaphs can range anywhere from the trite to the tragic. They can vary in tone from the whimsical "I told you I was sick!" to the poetic:

> The body of
> Benjamin Franklin, printer,
> (Like the cover of an old book,
> Its contents worn out,
> And stript of its lettering and gilding)
> Lies here, food for worms!
> Yet the work itself shall not be lost,
> For it will, as he believed, appear once more,
> In a new
> And more beautiful edition,
> Corrected and amended
> By its Author![1]

As we enter the cemetery of Old Testament characters, we come across the grave of a man of great accomplishment: Uzziah, king of Israel. Suddenly, however, we are struck by an overwhelming incongruity. Where we would have expected a pyramid built as a memorial, we find only a small, simple grave marker. Where we would have expected an eloquent eulogy chiseled in stone, we read only these words etched on his marker: "He is a leper."

How a man of Uzziah's monumental achievements came to be remembered so matter-of-factly, without feeling, without remorse, is the intriguing subject of our present study.

---

1. Benjamin Franklin in *The Oxford Book of American Literary Anecdotes,* ed. Donald Hall (New York, N.Y.: Oxford University Press, 1981), p. 13.

Uzziah as a Youth

After Solomon's death, the reins of the kingdom fell into the hands of his son—the greedy, power-hungry Rehoboam. Holding tight to those reins, he spurred people with sharp tax increases. Bucking his rule, the ten northern tribes slipped out from underneath the binding saddle of his throne and seceded to form an independent nation under Jeroboam. Consequently, Rehoboam was left to rule the two remaining tribes that he corralled to form the southern kingdom.

The tenth king down the line from Rehoboam was Uzziah, who ruled for fifty-two years, from 792–739 B.C. His was to be a path to prosperity—a path paved by parental influences.

> And all the people of Judah took Uzziah, who was sixteen years old, and made him king in the place of his father Amaziah. He built Eloth and restored it to Judah after the king slept with his fathers. Uzziah was sixteen years old when he became king, and he reigned fifty-two years in Jerusalem; and his mother's name was Jechiliah of Jerusalem. (2 Chron. 26:1–3)

We learn from 2 Chronicles 25:2a that Uzziah's father "did right in the sight of the Lord." Undoubtedly, his father's example provided the pavement on which Uzziah was to walk. However, the second half of the verse, "yet not with a whole heart," unearths the sharp stone in the road on which Uzziah would one day fall.

God does not take a divided heart lightly, to say the least. In fact, the clarion call trumpeted throughout the Old Testament and echoed in the New is:

> "You shall love the Lord your God with all your heart and with all your soul and with all your might." (Deut. 6:5)

The most sought-after territory on earth is not the oil fields of Saudi Arabia or the diamond mines of South Africa. It's your *heart*. Every past global war pales next to the white-hot battle being waged for your heart. For it, Satan gave up an eternity in heaven. For it, God gave up His only Son.

If you love God, but not with your whole heart . . . if you serve God, but not with your whole heart . . . then a portion of your heart is unclaimed territory—up for grabs. And, if you surrender even an isolated, insignificant beachhead to Satan, he has a foothold that may someday give him the advantage he needs to overthrow your loyalty to the Lord.

Won't you surrender to God and let Him unfurl His flag over *every* corner of your heart? A flag of the Lord's dominion over your life . . . to fly defiantly in the face of Satan . . . to fly colors unfurled so that others may see and rally behind it.

Following in his father's footsteps, Uzziah got off to a great start on his "Yellow Brick Road" to prosperity.

> And he did right in the sight of the Lord according to all that his father Amaziah had done. And he continued to seek God in the days of Zechariah, who had understanding through the vision of God; and as long as he sought the Lord, God prospered him. (2 Chron. 26:4–5)

Uzziah as a Statesman

The bricks to Uzziah's prosperity were gilded by the golden touch of God's blessing.

> Now he went out and warred against the Philistines, and broke down the wall of Gath and the wall of Jebneh and the wall of Ashdod; and he built cities in the area of Ashdod and among the Philistines. And God helped him against the Philistines, and against the Arabians who lived in Gur-baal, and the Meunites. The Ammonites also gave tribute to Uzziah, and his fame extended to the border of Egypt, for he became very strong. Moreover, Uzziah built towers in Jerusalem at the Corner Gate and at the Valley Gate and at the corner buttress and fortified them. And he built towers in the wilderness and hewed many cisterns, for he had much livestock, both in the lowland and in the plain. He also had plowmen and vinedressers in the hill country and the fertile fields, for he loved the soil. Moreover, Uzziah had an army ready for battle, which entered combat by divisions, according to the number of their muster, prepared by Jeiel the scribe and Maaseiah the official, under the direction of Hananiah, one of the king's officers. The total number of the heads of the

households, of valiant warriors, was 2,600. And under their direction was an elite army of 307,500, who could wage war with great power, to help the king against the enemy. Moreover, Uzziah prepared for all the army shields, spears, helmets, body armor, bows and sling stones. And in Jerusalem he made engines of war invented by skillful men to be on the towers and on the corners, for the purpose of shooting arrows and great stones. Hence his fame spread afar, for he was marvelously helped until he was strong. (vv. 6–15)

Politically, Uzziah's leadership resulted in triumph over his enemies (vv. 6–8) and great accomplishments in his kingdom (vv. 9–10). Militarily, he was organized, prepared (vv. 11–14), and inventive (v. 15). Personally, "his fame extended to the border of Egypt, for he became very strong" (v. 8b, see also v. 15b).

Uzziah as a Rebel

Tragically, Uzziah believed his own press clippings. As he skipped footloose through poppy fields of his own pride, Uzziah lost consciousness of the God who had helped him prosper.

> But when he became strong, his heart was so proud that he acted corruptly, and he was unfaithful to the Lord his God, for he entered the temple of the Lord to burn incense on the altar of incense. Then Azariah the priest entered after him and with him eighty priests of the Lord, valiant men. And they opposed Uzziah the king and said to him, "It is not for you, Uzziah, to burn incense to the Lord, but for the priests, the sons of Aaron who are consecrated to burn incense. Get out of the sanctuary, for you have been unfaithful, and will have no honor from the Lord God." (vv. 16–18)

In his book Mere Christianity, C. S. Lewis discusses man's greatest sin—pride.

> The essential vice, the utmost evil, is Pride. Unchastity, anger, greed, drunkenness, and all that, are mere fleabites in comparison: it was through Pride

that the devil became the devil: Pride leads to every other vice: it is the complete anti-God state of mind. . . . As long as you are proud you cannot know God. A proud man is always looking down on things and people: and, of course, as long as you are looking down, you cannot see something that is above you.[2]

Uzziah as a Leper

Preening over his strength, Uzziah believed himself to be bigger than life, thus totally crowding God out of the scene. And like a narcissistic movie star with an inflated ego, Uzziah was vulnerably poised for the critic's pinprick.

> But Uzziah, with a censer in his hand for burning incense, was enraged; and while he was enraged with the priests, the leprosy broke out on his forehead before the priests in the house of the Lord, beside the altar of incense. And Azariah the chief priest and all the priests looked at him, and behold, he was leprous on his forehead; and they hurried him out of there, and he himself also hastened to get out because the Lord had smitten him. And King Uzziah was a leper to the day of his death; and he lived in a separate house, being a leper, for he was cut off from the house of the Lord. And Jotham his son was over the king's house judging the people of the land. Now the rest of the acts of Uzziah, first to last, the prophet Isaiah, the son of Amoz, has written. So Uzziah slept with his fathers, and they buried him with his fathers in the field of the grave which belonged to the kings, for they said, "He is a leper." And Jotham his son became king in his place. (vv. 19–23)

A Closing Epitaph

The words "He is a leper" are chiseled into the cold granite memory of Scripture as a tragic epitaph to one whose fame once reached the very borders of the mighty Egyptian empire. Hawthorne

---

2. *A Mind Awake: An Anthology of C. S. Lewis,* ed. Clyde S. Kilby (New York, N.Y.: Harcourt, Brace and World, 1969), p. 115.

was correct when he said: "A grave, wherever it is found, preaches a short and pithy sermon to the soul."[3] If you died today, what words would etch your tombstone? What sermon would those words preach about your life?

🍇 *Living Insights*

Some very practical theology surfaces in this study—not the least of which is learning to deal with *success.* You might think, "I'd give anything just to have success! Don't worry, I'll deal with it!" These are often famous last words. Let's discuss the following observations.

• *No genuine success is possible apart from the Lord.* Do you agree with this principle? Why?

_____

_____

How do you explain those ungodly people around you who seem outwardly successful?

_____

_____

Is there a formula for success? If so, what is it? If not, why not?

_____

_____

_____

• *There are few tests like the one success brings.* Have you personally been put to this test? How did you handle it?

_____

_____

_____

_____

3. Nathaniel Hawthorne in *1,001 Sermon Illustrations and Quotations,* comp. Geikie, Cowper, and others (Grand Rapids, Mich.: Baker Book House, 1954), p. 54.

Do you know others put to this test? How did they handle it?

_____

_____

_____

_____

• *The Lord who blesses us is also able to bruise and break us.* Can you back up this principle with Scripture references? Share them.

_____

_____

_____

Why would God want to bruise or break us?

_____

_____

_____

Where are you in this whole process?

_____

_____

_____

🍇 Living Insights   STUDY TWO

Prosperity followed Uzziah as long as he sought the Lord (26:5). Paraphrase these verses from Psalms that exhort us to seek the Lord.

9:10 _____

_____

22:26 _____

_____

24:6 _____

_____

34:10 _____

_____

70:4 _____

_____

105:3 _____

_____

Although we may recognize Him as our refuge, our strength, and our source of blessing, once prosperity comes, it's easy to focus on blessing in the foreground rather than His hand in the background. When that happens, the only hand we see in the picture is ours, thus preparing the way for pride. God's warning to the Israelites before they entered into the blessings of the Promised Land serves to correct our vision.

> Beware lest you forget the Lord your God . . . lest, when you have eaten and are satisfied . . . and when your herds and your flocks multiply, and your silver and gold multiply, and all that you have multiplies, then your heart becomes proud, and you forget the Lord your God who brought you out from the land of Egypt, out of the house of slavery. He led you through the great and terrible wilderness, with its fiery serpents and scorpions and thirsty ground where there was no water; He brought water for you out of the rock of flint. In the wilderness He fed you manna which your fathers did not know, that He might humble you and that He might test you, to do good for you in the end. Otherwise, you may say in your heart, 'My power and the strength of my hand made me this wealth.' But you shall remember the Lord your God, for it is He who is giving you power to make wealth." (Deut. 8:11–18a)

Look around at your blessings—family, health, friends, home, job, material possessions. Jot down several of the specific blessings in your own life.

_____

_____

_____

_____

_____

_____

_____

_____

_____

_____

_____

Whose hand do you see providing them? If you have to squint to see God's hand, maybe it's time to readjust your focus. Remember: "*In Him* we live and move and exist" (Acts 17:28, emphasis added). Conversely, *without Him,* we would be able to do nothing. Therefore, *to Him,* and Him alone, should go the glory and praise.

Chapter 9

FROM CAPTIVE TO QUEEN: AN ADOPTION STORY

Romans 8, Galatians 4, Esther

Most of us haven't had to look abortion in the eyes. We read about it, shudder at the thought of it, even campaign against it. But we never really get close enough to see its blackness. Only the few who enclose themselves within the cold, clean walls to watch the act . . . only they understand what really happens. One surgeon, a pro-life advocate, poignantly expresses his reaction to witnessing an abortion.

> I know. We cannot feed the great numbers. There is no more room. I know, I know. It is a woman's right to refuse the risk, to decline the pain of child-birth. And an unwanted child is a very great burden. An unwanted child is a burden to himself. I know.
>
> And yet . . . there is the flick of that needle. I *saw* it. I saw . . . I *felt*—in that room, a pace away, life prodded, life fending off. I saw life avulsed—swept by flood, blackening—then *out.*
>
> There, says the doctor. It's all over. It wasn't too bad, was it? he says to the woman.
>
> She smiles. It is all over. Oh, yes.
>
> And who would care to imagine that from a moist and dark commencement six months before there would ripen the cluster and globule, the sprout and pouch of man?[1]

The purpose of this lesson is not to dwell on the atrocity of abortion, the cruelty of man—the dark side. Rather, it is to radiate the alternative—the light and warmth of adoption. It extends the hand of salvation to all involved.

When an adoptive couple finally holds a child in their arms—their child—they are saved from the anxiety of waiting or the anguish of infertility. It's as if the living, breathing bundle instantly

---

1. Richard Selzer, *Mortal Lessons* (New York, N.Y.: Simon and Schuster, 1976), pp. 159–60.

soothes their pain. And the child is saved too—perhaps from being unwanted, or raised by incompetent parents, or thoughtlessly snuffed out.

Adoption is God's candle in the black abysses of childlessness and abortion.

In this lesson we will see how God used Esther's adoption to raise her status from an orphaned captive to a beloved queen. Likewise, we will learn how we have been lifted from hell's pit to be joint heirs with the King.

The Theology of Adoption

Romans 8 is the *magnum opus*, the *sine qua non* of Paul's theological statement about life with God. Specifically, Paul talks about some of the benefits of being connected with God's family (vv. 1–15).

First, we are protected *forever* from God's condemnation (v. 1). Second, we are set free from the oppressive bondage of sin and death (v. 2). Third, we receive the power of the Holy Spirit, which enables us to spurn the flesh and walk "according to the Spirit" (v. 4). Fourth, we gain the mind of the Spirit, which is "life and peace" (v. 6). Fifth, we have the righteousness of God (v. 10). Sixth, we have assurance that we will be resurrected from the dead (v. 13). Galatians 4 underscores these rich truths about adoption:

> God sent forth His Son, born of a woman, born
> under the Law, in order that He might redeem those
> who were under the Law, that we might receive the
> adoption[2] as sons. (vv. 4b–5)

In other words, God reaches into the slave market of sin, breaks our fetters, and redeems[3] us as we come to Him by faith. We are no longer slaves, but sons and heirs through God (v. 7); we are entitled to a wealth of privileges and responsibilities.

---

2. The term *adoption* is a rich one. It comes from a combination of two Greek words: *huios*, meaning "son," and *tithēmi*, which means "to sit, to place, to put." The result is the term *huiothesia*, which means "the placement of a son." For more references to adoption, see Romans 9:4 and Ephesians 1:5.

3. The Greek word for *redemption* is used of the price of redeeming something that is in pawn, of the money paid to ransom prisoners of war, and of money paid to buy a slave's freedom. Titus 2:13b–14 lists the price of our salvation: " . . . our great God and Savior, Christ Jesus; who gave *Himself* for us" (emphasis added). For more references on redemption, see Mark 10:45, 1 Timothy 2:6, and Romans 3:24. Also see *The Apostolic Preaching of the Cross*, by Leon Morris (Grand Rapids, Mich.: William B. Eerdmans Publishing Co., 1960), pp. 9–59.

Strangely, many of us who have accepted God's offer of salvation are still trying to find a way to pay Him back. We come to God with one hand extended, and the other groping around in our front pocket for loose change. It's our instinct to want to pay our debts—to even things up. After all, we've got to be responsible.

Have you let the "if anyone will not work, neither let him eat" principle infect your theology (2 Thess. 3:10b)? Do you think that the more church committees you belong to, Sunday school classes you teach, Third World children you sponsor, the more worthy you'll be of God's gift of eternal life?

The gift *did* come at a great price—God's only begotten Son. But to us, it comes free—without strings or buy-now, pay-later conditions. It's been paid for . . . *totally* . . . by Jesus.

A Biography of Adoption

Biographically, the Book of Esther illustrates the theological truth of adoption. Esther was a young Jewish woman who was orphaned, then mercifully adopted by her cousin Mordecai (2:5–7). This drama stars three more characters: Ahasuerus, king of Persia, also known as Xerxes; Vashti, the king's beautiful wife; and Haman, the one who wears the black hat. Out of the sixty-six books in the Bible, Esther is the only one that doesn't mention the name of God. But even though His name is absent, His providential fingerprints can be found throughout.[4] Replete with action and intrigue, this ancient story of adoption still speaks to us.

A Feast Marked by Punishment

King Ahasuerus threw a big bash for the entire populace of Susa, the capital city of the Persian Empire (1:5). During the seven days of this revelry, "the royal wine was plentiful according to the king's bounty" (v. 7). On the seventh day, when "the king was merry with wine," he decided to send for Queen Vashti to come in and parade her beauty in front of his guests (vv. 10–11).

But Vashti said no, which in her day was not a popular thing to do. Many modern women would have applauded Vashti's liber-

---

4. Too often, if God's name isn't billboarded in front of us, we can't see Him . . . can't feel the warmth of His breath. But God doesn't always advertise His presence. Sometimes, He only whispers it. He wants us to be sensitive to His subtle ways. Just as Adam and Eve heard the sound of God walking in the garden (Gen. 3:8), we also need to put our ears to the ground and listen for the silent thunder of His gentle footsteps as He sovereignly walks the earth.

ated conduct, but not King Ahasuerus. He was so angry, his wrath burned so within him, that he sought counsel on what disciplinary measures he should take with Vashti (vv. 12–15). Concerned that the queen's rebelliousness would license the other married women in the Persian kingdom to disobey their husbands, the king was advised to ban her from his presence and replace her with a more deserving woman.

An Ancient Beauty Contest

To find Vashti's replacement, the king staged a beauty pageant. The entire kingdom was scoured so he could choose the most beautiful young virgin. Mordecai entered Esther in the contest, advising her not to reveal her Jewish background. And as the finger of God began to move through the streets of Susa, it landed sovereignly on Esther.

> And the king loved Esther more than all the women, and she found favor and kindness with him more than all the virgins, so that he set the royal crown on her head and made her queen instead of Vashti. (2:17)

A Crucial Subplot

After this climactic scene, the camera seems to wander inadvertently to an extraneous subplot. In this Alfred Hitchcock scene, Mordecai learned of a plot to assassinate the king and reported it to Esther, who then informed the king "in Mordecai's name" (v. 22). After a thorough investigation, Mordecai's information is verified, the two conspirators are hung, and it is "written in the Book of the Chronicles in the king's presence" (v. 23). Tuck this scene away in your mind until later. After seeing God's sovereign hand, we will understand its significance.

A Promotion and a Plot

Meanwhile, Haman is promoted to the king's right-hand man, and the king commanded everyone to pay homage to Haman. But Mordecai, aware of Haman's greed and conceit, "neither bowed down nor paid homage" (3:2b). And he was not about to be excused from such disobedience.

> When Haman saw that Mordecai neither bowed down nor paid homage to him, Haman was filled with rage. But he disdained to lay hands on Mordecai alone,

for they had told him who the people of Mordecai were; therefore Haman sought to destroy all the Jews, the people of Mordecai, who were throughout the whole kingdom of Ahasuerus. (vv. 5–6)

An ancient holocaust took shape in the mind of this Old Testament Hitler. In verses 8 and 9, Haman unveils his plot to the king.

Then Haman said to King Ahasuerus, "There is a certain people scattered and dispersed among the peoples in all the provinces of your kingdom; their laws are different from those of all other people, and they do not observe the king's laws, so it is not in the king's interest to let them remain. If it is pleasing to the king, let it be decreed that they be destroyed, and I will pay ten thousand talents of silver into the hands of those who carry on the king's business, to put into the king's treasuries."

The king's response undoubtedly made Haman grin:

Then the king took his signet ring from his hand and gave it to Haman, . . . the enemy of the Jews. And the king said to Haman, "The silver is yours, and the people also, to do with them as you please." (vv. 10–11)

A Creative Plan

After discovering Haman's plot, Mordecai and all the people mourn (4:1–3). When Esther hears of the plot, she inquires about the details but stops short of offering any real help (vv. 4–12). Mordecai then sends this convicting word by way of a messenger:

"Do not imagine that you in the king's palace can escape any more than all the Jews. For if you remain silent at this time, relief and deliverance will arise for the Jews from another place and you and your father's house will perish. And who knows whether you have not attained royalty for such a time as this?" (4:13–14)

Talk about great rhetoric! It's as if Mordecai is saying, "This is your meeting with destiny, Esther. This is why God had me take you as a little girl and rear you His way. This is God's work. Don't be silent. Speak up!" And Esther gave this reply to Mordecai:

> "Go, assemble all the Jews who are found in Susa, and fast for me; do not eat or drink for three days, night or day. I and my maidens also will fast in the same way. And thus I will go in to the king, which is not according to the law; and if I perish, I perish." (v. 16)

Risking her life, Esther comes before the king without a summons. He openly welcomes her into his presence and beckons her to make her request. She puts the king off momentarily, inviting him and Haman to a banquet she had prepared. While dining together, she invites them to a banquet on the next day, when she promises to reveal her request (5:1–8).

Pleased with being considered part of the royalty, his head swelling with pride, Haman leaves the feast. However, his good feelings are squelched at the sight of Mordecai, who still refuses to bow down to him. Enraged, Haman plots to have Mordecai hanged the next morning (5:9–14).

Before we get swept away by the unfolding drama of the story, let's take a moment to get a close-up of Esther. On the old metal scale that measures faith against works, Esther weighs in evenly. Notice her well-balanced response to Mordecai's plea. Notice how she asks the Jews to fast with her for three days, to display externally the seriousness of their prayers to God—stacking the weight on the works side. Notice also her words, "If I perish, I perish" (4:16), which demonstrate her firm confidence in God's plan—adding weight to the faith side.

It's true. God's gift of salvation is free—received by faith alone. But our works are its vital signs, proof that our faith is alive and active (see James 2:17–18). Take a look at the New Testament scale in perfect balance:

> For by grace you have been saved through faith; and that not of yourselves, *it is the gift of God; not as a result of works,* that no one should boast. For we are His workmanship, *created in Christ Jesus for good works,* which God prepared beforehand, that we should walk in them. (Eph. 2:8–10, emphasis added)

Is the faith pan of your spiritual scale scraping the tabletop, while the works pan hangs elevated and empty? Or is your scale tipped toward the works tray, leaving the faith tray sorely wanting?

A Reading of Remembrance and Overdue Honor

That night, while the gallows were being built, King Ahasuerus couldn't sleep, "so he gave an order to bring the book of records, the chronicles, and they were read before the king" (Esther 6:1). Reminded that Mordecai had tipped him off about the conspiracy, King Ahasuerus decides to honor him. So the king sends for Haman and asks, "What is to be done for the man whom the king desires to honor?" (v. 6). Certain that the king wants to honor *him*, Haman answers:

> "For the man whom the king desires to honor, let them bring a royal robe which the king has worn, and the horse on which the king has ridden, and on whose head a royal crown has been placed; and let the robe and the horse be handed over to one of the king's most noble princes and let them array the man whom the king desires to honor and lead him on horseback through the city square, and proclaim before him, 'Thus it shall be done to the man whom the king desires to honor.' " (vv. 7b–9)[5]

The king takes this advice. But to Haman's shame, *he* has to honor Mordecai. What dramatic irony! After carrying out the king's wishes, Haman "hurried home, mourning, with his head covered" (v. 12).

Exposure and Justice

That evening, at Esther's banquet, the king again asks Esther to reveal her request.

> Then Queen Esther answered and said, "If I have found favor in your sight, O king, and if it please the king, let my life be given me as my petition, and my people as my request; for we have been sold, I and my people, to be destroyed, to be killed and to be annihilated. Now if we had only been sold as

---

5. Theologian Merrill Unger makes an interesting comment on Haman's pride. "What an illustration of the truth that 'pride goeth before destruction, and an haughty spirit before a fall' (Prov. 16:18; cf. 18:12). The honors Haman's pride would bestow upon himself were to be bestowed upon his enemy, Mordecai, the Jew, hatred for whom had deprived him of all sense and reason, and like all his ilk, made him a colossal megalomaniac." Merrill F. Unger, *Unger's Commentary on the Old Testament* (Chicago, Ill.: Moody Press, 1981), vol. 1, p. 665.

slaves, men and women, I would have remained silent, for the trouble would not be commensurate with the annoyance to the king." (7:3–4)

The king asks Esther, "Who is he, and where is he, who would presume to do thus?" (v. 5). Esther responds, "A foe and an enemy, is this wicked Haman!" (v. 6). The king, outraged, had Haman hung on the very gallows he had built to execute Mordecai. Haman's plot to destroy the Jews was foiled because of Esther's courage—an adopted woman who risked her life to save her people. The book closes with the Feast of Purim ("Peace"), which is still celebrated by the Jews in Esther's honor (8:1–10:3).

The Practicality of Adoption

Esther's story illustrates the beauty not only of spiritual adoption but of physical adoption as well. Remembering these three truths will help us see the unique significance of adoption.

First: *The adoption process best models the way people enter God's family.* Families with adopted children are living illustrations of salvation. Like adoptive parents, who reach into humanity and *choose* a child—and not on the child's merit—God has mercifully reached out and said, "You're unique, and you're Mine."

Second: *Adopted children often become God's special instruments.* As He did with Esther, God sometimes chooses adopted children to fulfill His special purposes. Their destinies have been changed; many have been preserved, rescued from dire circumstances to fulfill God's purposes in the light of His love.

Third: *People who are touched by the adopted realize how profound God's plan is.* If you've brushed lives with adopted children, you understand the graciousness of God's redemptive design.

Throughout the story of Esther, we see so clearly God's sovereign plan of salvation. With hindsight, we can see His hand in each detail of the story. Separately, each detail is a disjointed pearl. But God took this pile of pearls, strung them together, and added a clasp to create something beautiful and useful.

Like an adopted child—who was not aborted but allowed to live—our destinies were altered when we became part of God's family. The individual pearls of our lives have been threaded together to form a life of purpose and meaning. We have been saved from the death we were headed for and have been chosen instead to live.

Living Insights

STUDY ONE

The story of Queen Esther is a fascinating one. Even though it may be in one of the dustier portions of your Bible, this dramatic account is rich in truth.

For today's study, imagine you are a cub reporter for the *Persian Post*. Your first assignment is to cover the story of the captive who became a queen. Read through Esther 1–7. The following will help you ask all the questions you'll need to write your article. Be sure to get all the facts—we want to keep you on at this newspaper!

From Captive to Queen: Esther 1–7

Who? _____

_____

What? _____

_____

When? _____

_____

Where? _____

_____

Why? _____

_____

How? _____

_____

Living Insights

STUDY TWO

People have many different thoughts and feelings about adoption. Some people are excited about being adopted; others seem to pity children who are adopted. How do you feel about it? Let's see.

What are the similarities between natural birth and adoption?

_____

_____

What are the differences?

_____

_____

What advantages do adopted people enjoy?

_____

_____

_____

What disadvantages do they live with?

_____

_____

_____

Do you treat adopted children differently? Why or why not?

_____

_____

_____

How do you treat couples who want to adopt?

_____

_____

_____

What can you learn from the theology of spiritual adoption to help you understand and appreciate adoption in the physical realm?

_____

_____

_____

_____

How Are We to Understand the Book?

Turning our attention from the person of Jonah to the Book of Jonah[2] is like turning our faces to the biting winds of a severe storm. No book in the Bible has been as badly battered by a sea of criticism as Jonah. Some people believe the book is a parable—an earthly story with a heavenly meaning—similar to the story of the Prodigal Son (Luke 15:11–32). But this view disregards the fact that Christ, in the same book (11:29–30), regards Jonah as a historical person.

Some see the book as allegory, like John Bunyan's *Pilgrim's Progress*, where the story's true meaning can only be found by translating its characters and events into the truths they symbolize. Jonah's narrative, however, lacks the obvious allegorical signposts of *Pilgrim's Progress*, where Christian encounters such characters as Great Despair and Mr. Worldly Wiseman on his journey to the Celestial City. In Jonah, all the signs are posted along real routes traveled by real people on their way to real cities.

The final interpretative option is to accept the book at face value—as a historical narrative.[3] The traditional explanation has been questioned in modern times due to the miraculous nature of the book's events. Consequently, if you reject the miraculous from the outset, you have to reject the book's historical character as well. But if you accept the miraculous intervention of God in human events, then accepting the book as a straightforward historical account should pose no problem. Certainly, if you accept the miracle of the fish and loaves, then the miracle of the fish and Jonah shouldn't be too hard to swallow!

To understand the book's message, we need to cast a net that catches the essentials and allows the incidentals to slip away. The message is not the story of a man swallowed by a fish. It is an account of how God dealt with a reluctant and recalcitrant prophet who stubbornly refused to obey Him in carrying His Word to Israel's enemy. When we draw the net tighter, these incidental fingerlings

---

2. Scholars have argued from Jonah 1:1 that the book never states it is Jonah's autobiography. But the autobiographical accounts of Hosea, Joel, Micah, Zephaniah, Haggai, Zechariah, and Malachi begin in a similar way.

3. The historical places referred to are Nineveh (1:2), Tarshish, and Joppa (v. 3). Furthermore, the population of Nineveh, approximated by some scholars to be 600,000 (based on a population of more than 120,000 children in 4:11), is substantiated by archaeological evidence. See *The Biblical World: A Dictionary of Biblical Archaeology*, ed. Charles F. Pfeiffer (Grand Rapids, Mich.: Baker Book House, 1966), pp. 415–17.

slip back into the water: the ship . . . the sea . . . the fish . . . the dry land . . . the plant . . . the worm.

The story of Jonah becomes evident when we divide it into four parts. In chapter 1, he's running *from* God; in chapter 2, he's running *to* God; in chapter 3, he's running *with* God; in chapter 4, he's running *against* God.

Why Didn't Jonah Want to Go to Nineveh?

What would cause God's prophet to flee from His presence? Most commentators list three reasons: fear, prejudice, and pride. Some say Jonah feared stepping into enemy land. This is doubtful because he was not afraid to board the ship—there is no word that he feared the storm, no hint that he feared dying at sea. Others say that since Jonah was a Jew, he didn't want to lower himself to taking a message from God to the Gentiles. While on board, however, he expressed a deep compassion for the welfare of the idol-worshiping sailors, telling them to toss him overboard if they wanted to stop the storm. Still others say pride kept Jonah from going to Nineveh. If he went declaring a message of judgment and the people repented, God would show mercy, and Jonah's prophecy would be null and void. His credentials as a prophet in Jeroboam's court would then be greatly devalued if not bankrupt altogether.

Why didn't Jonah want to go to Nineveh? The answer is found in chapter 4, verse 2. Jonah clearly states that he fled to Tarshish because he knew God would show the Ninevites mercy if they repented.

> "Therefore, in order to forestall this I fled to Tarshish, for I knew that Thou art a gracious and compassionate God, slow to anger and abundant in lovingkindness, and one who relents concerning calamity."

Their cup of wickedness was full . . . their days were numbered . . . their doom was certain. This was fine with Jonah, as Nineveh was a mistress kingdom to the powerful empire of Assyria, Israel's arch-enemy.[4] Assyria was a brutal foe, a barbarous people with a

4. Nineveh, the capital of Assyria since the time of Sennacherib, embodied human self-exaltation. Brutal in warfare, barbaric in the slaughter of his captives, Sennacherib called himself "the great king" (2 Kings 18:28) and arrogantly thought of himself as a self-made military genius in his program of world conquest (Isa. 10:12–14). These are the associations that probably came to Jonah's mind when he thought of Nineveh. Jonah undoubtedly shared Nahum's sentiments about Nineveh's downfall in 612 B.C. "Woe to the bloody city, completely full of lies and pillage. . . . Nineveh is devastated! Who will grieve for her? . . . All who hear about you Will clap their hands over you, For on whom has not your evil passed continually?" (Nahum 3:1, 7, and 19).

horrible mania for blood and vengeance. It is no wonder that Jonah wanted them destroyed.

Did a Whale Actually Swallow Jonah?

The next bit of introductory baggage deals with the whale in our tale. First, the text says the whale was "appointed" by God (1:17). The term is never used in the sense of creating but of *assigning* or *ordaining*.[5] Second, note that the phrase "great fish" was used instead of the word *whale*.[6] What's in view here is probably a whale shark, which grows to enormous proportions and is not, by nature, a man-eater.

But could an enormous fish—whale or otherwise—really swallow a whole man? In his commentary on Jonah, C. F. Keil notes one such instance with a shark and a sailor.[7] Interpreting the "great fish" of Jonah 1:17 to possibly mean a whale, R. K. Harrison notes several reported cases of whales swallowing men alive.

> As regards the credibility of the event described, it has frequently been remarked that the true whale has such a narrow gullet that it could only swallow comparatively small fish, and certainly nothing approaching the size of a man. In this general connection, however, it is important to observe that the Hebrew spoke of a "great fish" (Jon. 1:17), that is to say, some kind of sea denizen, and that the interpretation "whale" is the result of translations into English. Furthermore, while the true whale, whose habitat is the Arctic Ocean rather than the Mediterranean Sea, cannot swallow a man, the sperm whale or *cachalot* most probably can. Despite this constitutional obstacle it was shown as long ago as 1915 that even a true whale could save a man from drowning if he managed to negotiate the air-supply tract of the mammal and reach the great laryngeal pouch. . . . On another occasion a whale-hunter was

5. The Hebrew term is *manah*.

6. The Hebrew term *dag gadol* literally means "great fish." In the New Testament, this term is translated *kētos*, meaning "sea monster" (see Matt. 12:40).

7. C. F. Keil, *Minor Prophets*, vol. 10 of *Commentary on the Old Testament in Ten Volumes* (Grand Rapids, Mich.: William B. Eerdmans Publishing Co., n.d.), p. 398.

reportedly swallowed in 1891, but was recovered the
following day in unconscious condition from the inside of the mammal. Again, a seaman was said to
have been swallowed by a large sperm whale in the
vicinity of the Falkland Islands, and after three days
was recovered unconscious but alive, though with
some damage to his skin.[8]

Whether the "great fish" was a whale, a whale shark, or some
other sea creature, the great miracle of Jonah was not that he was
swallowed or that he was kept alive for three days. The miracle was
the Ninevites' response to the message Jonah preached. One and
all, great and small, they repented and transferred their allegiance
to the one true "Great King"—the Lord of hosts.

A miracle like that can happen in your life—right now—as you
read this. God can touch your heart, and with His compassion,
change your life as He changed the lives of the Ninevites.

 Living Insights   STUDY ONE

This lesson gives us a wonderful overview of the Book of Jonah.
Actually, the entire story is explained in forty-eight verses. Let's
take a look at it paragraph by paragraph.

The following list divides the book into eleven paragraphs. Read
each passage slowly and carefully. Next to its reference, give each
paragraph a title. It will take some thought, but have fun with this
project. And by all means, be creative!

Overview of Jonah

1:1–3 _____

1:4–9 _____

1:10–14 _____

1:15–17 _____

2:1–9 _____

8. Roland Kenneth Harrison, *Introduction to the Old Testament* (Grand Rapids, Mich.:
William B. Eerdmans Publishing Co., 1969), p. 907, as originally quoted from the following
sources: G. Macloskie, *Bibliotheca Sacra*, vol. 72 (1915) p. 336f; *Neue Lutheranische Kirchenzeitung*
(1895) p. 303; A. J. Wilson, *Princeton Theological Review*, vol. 25 (1927) p. 636.

2:10 _____

3:1–4 _____

3:5–10 _____

4:1–4 _____

4:5–8 _____

4:9–11 _____

🍇 Living Insights   STUDY TWO

The greatest miracle in the Book of Jonah is not the incident with the "great fish." The greatest miracle is one of the most successful evangelistic crusades in the history of the world. Let's get a little closer to home. How does Jonah's life compare with yours?

How open are you to sharing the gospel to the ends of the earth?

_____

_____

Are there religious, cultural, or economic roadblocks that cause you to detour around certain people?

_____

_____

How can you overcome this attitude and fulfill our Lord's great commission?

_____

_____

_____

As you ponder these questions, ask God to guide you to those who need to hear about Him. If you commit this to prayer now, you can avoid the fish's belly later!

Chapter 11

THE PRODIGAL PREACHER

Jonah 1–2

The first two chapters of Jonah show how God dealt with the disobedience of one of His messengers. Like a wanted poster, these chapters depict Jonah as a fugitive. In a sermon on Jonah in the book *Moby Dick,* Father Mapple describes this runaway prophet.

> "With this sin of disobedience in him, Jonah still further flouts at God, by seeking to flee from Him. He thinks that a ship made by men will carry him into countries where God does not reign, but only the Captains of this earth. He skulks about the wharves of Joppa, seeks a ship that's bound for Tarshish. . . . Miserable man! Oh! most contemptible and worthy of all scorn; with slouched hat and guilty eye, skulking from his God; prowling among the shipping like a vile burglar hastening to cross the seas. So disordered, self-condemning is his look, that had there been policemen in those days, Jonah, on the mere suspicion of something wrong, had been arrested ere he touched a deck. How plainly he's a fugitive! No baggage, not a hat-box, valise, or carpet-bag—no friends accompany him to the wharf with their adieux."[1]

Such is the sad, shadowy picture of a man going to great lengths to run from God. But as we shall see in this lesson, God will go to even greater lengths to retrieve him.

God's Command

The book begins in a dramatic and arresting way as God breaks the silence of heaven to give Jonah his missionary orders.

> The word of the Lord came to Jonah the son of Amittai saying, "Arise, go to Nineveh the great city,

---

1. Herman Melville, *Moby Dick; or, The Whale,* in vol. 48 of *Great Books of the Western World,* ed. Robert Maynard Hutchins (Chicago, Ill.: Encyclopaedia Britannica, 1971), p. 31.

and cry against it, for their wickedness has come up
before Me." (1:1–2)

Traveling and preaching usually posed no problem for prophets.
That was their job. But in this case, something churned Jonah's
stomach—Nineveh. The very sound of it sickened him, because it
was the capital of the vicious and godless Assyrians, Israel's arch-
enemy. In every city they conquered, the Assyrians built a pyramid
of human skulls. That was the brutal business card they left behind,
and that was why Jonah responded as he did.

Jonah's Disobedience

From Jonah's perspective, God had gone too far. He was asking
too much. So instead of arising . . . going . . . and crying out,
Jonah arose . . . fled . . . and shipped out.[2]

> But Jonah rose up to flee to Tarshish from the pres-
> ence of the Lord. So he went down to Joppa, found
> a ship which was going to Tarshish, paid the fare,
> and went down into it to go with them to Tarshish
> from the presence of the Lord. (v. 3)

Are you, like Jonah, in the process of fleeing from the presence
of God because He is asking you to do something that is just *too*
much? Fleeing from the Lord is like trying to draw a round square.
It's a logical impossibility. God is omnipresent—everywhere—and
you can't escape from Someone who is everywhere.

> Where can I go from Thy Spirit?
> Or where can I flee from Thy presence?
> If I ascend to heaven, Thou art there;
> If I make my bed in Sheol, behold, Thou art there.
> If I take the wings of the dawn,
> If I dwell in the remotest part of the sea,
> Even there Thy hand will lead me,
> And Thy right hand will lay hold of me.
> If I say, "Surely the darkness will overwhelm me,
> And the light around me will be night,"
> Even the darkness is not dark to Thee,

2. Tarshish was two thousand miles away from Nineveh and was the westernmost point on
any trade route.

And the night is as bright as the day.
Darkness and light are alike to Thee. (Ps. 139:7–12)

Whether you're on a raft in the middle of the ocean or in a cave in the cliffs of some mountain—He is there. Whether you are adrift in a sea of immorality or you have a heart that is hidden, distant, and cold—He is there.

God's Response to Jonah's Disobedience

God's plan to deliver Nineveh (see 2 Pet. 3:9) was not thwarted by a stubborn, strong-willed prophet, regardless of his credentials. God harnessed the wild winds of nature to hunt down this fugitive from faithfulness.

> And the Lord hurled a great wind on the sea and there was a great storm on the sea so that the ship was about to break up. (Jon. 1:4)

When we're disobedient to God, our actions often have a negative effect, bringing a storm into our lives that can shipwreck the lives of those around us. But the storm God sends is not meant to sweep us away but to bring us home. Notice how God's hunt for the prodigal prophet is tenaciously active. "The Lord *hurled* a great wind" (emphasis added). God has his own way of bringing lost sheep back into His fold and will go to the ends of the earth and the depths of the oceans to do it. Apparently, the storm was so great that even the seasoned sailors on board feared for their lives and resorted to drastic measures.

> Then the sailors became afraid, and every man cried to his god, and they threw the cargo which was in the ship into the sea to lighten it for them. But Jonah had gone below into the hold of the ship, lain down, and fallen sound asleep. (v. 5)

It is said that there are no atheists at sea, and these sailors give evidence of that. Notice, however, where Jonah is. Safe below, sound asleep. But the frenzied captain soon changes all that.

> So the captain approached him and said, "How is it that you are sleeping? Get up, call on your god. Perhaps your god will be concerned about us so that we will not perish." And each man said to his mate, "Come, let us cast lots so we may learn on whose

account this calamity has struck us." So they cast lots and the lot fell on Jonah. Then they said to him, "Tell us, now! On whose account has this calamity struck us? What is your occupation? And where do you come from? What is your country? From what people are you?" (vv. 6–8)

With the finger of accusation pointed at Jonah, the prophet reveals his identity and testifies.

And he said to them, "I am a Hebrew, and I fear the Lord God of heaven who made the sea and the dry land." (v. 9)

Immediately, the sailors put this missing piece of information into the puzzle of the sudden storm.

Then the men became extremely frightened and they said to him, "How could you do this?" For the men knew that he was fleeing from the presence of the Lord, because he had told them. (v. 10)

Desperately, the sailors plead with Jonah for a way to calm the storm.

So they said to him, "What should we do to you that the sea may become calm for us?"—for the sea was becoming increasingly stormy. And he said to them, "Pick me up and throw me into the sea. Then the sea will become calm for you, for I know that on account of me this great storm has come upon you." However, the men rowed desperately to return to land but they could not, for the sea was becoming even stormier against them. (vv. 11–13)

Hesitant to take a man's life, the sailors try to ride out the storm. Finally, exhausting their human effort at the oars, the unbelieving sailors turn to God.

Then they called on the Lord and said, "We earnestly pray, O Lord, do not let us perish on account of this man's life and do not put innocent blood on us; for Thou, O Lord, hast done as Thou hast pleased." So they picked up Jonah, threw him into the sea, and the sea stopped its raging. (vv. 14–15)

The miraculous calming of the sea created an equally miraculous change in the lives of the sailors.

> Then the men feared the Lord greatly, and they offered a sacrifice to the Lord and made vows. (v. 16)

God's Salvation

God's salvation not only extends to the pagans in a spiritual sense, but goes even further to save the prophet in a physical sense. God does not abandon Jonah, regardless of his disobedience, but in an act of grace snatches him safely away.

> And the Lord appointed a great fish to swallow Jonah, and Jonah was in the stomach of the fish three days and three nights. (v. 17)

The brief description of Jonah's ordeal "in the stomach of the fish three days and three nights" is crisp and clean. But if you use your imagination to recreate the scene, it will terrify you.

Pitch black. Sloshing gastric juices wash over you, burning skin, eyes, throat, nostrils. Oxygen is scarce and each frantic gulp of air is saturated with salt water. The rancid smell of digested food causes you to throw up repeatedly until you have only dry heaves left. Everything you touch has the slimy feel of the mucous membrane that lines the stomach. You feel claustrophobic. With every turn and dive of the great fish, you slip and slide in the cesspool of digestive fluid. There are no footholds. No blankets to keep you warm from the cold, clammy depths of the sea.

For three days and three nights you endure this harsh womb of God's grace. His grace sometimes comes to us in ways we would never expect. Does God have you in the stomach of some dark, slippery, distasteful circumstances? If so, prayer is the only lamp by which you will see through the darkness and to the Savior's grace.

Jonah's Prayer

From the murky depths of despair, Jonah calls out to God for deliverance.

> Then Jonah prayed to the Lord his God from the
> stomach of the fish, and he said,
> "I called out of my distress to the Lord,
> And He answered me.

I cried for help from the depth of Sheol;
Thou didst hear my voice.
For Thou hadst cast me into the deep,
Into the heart of the seas,
And the current engulfed me.
All Thy breakers and billows passed over me.
So I said, 'I have been expelled from Thy
sight.
Nevertheless I will look again toward Thy
holy temple.'
Water encompassed me to the point of
death.
The great deep engulfed me,
Weeds were wrapped around my head.
I descended to the roots of the mountains.
The earth with its bars was around me
forever,
But Thou hast brought up my life from the
pit, O Lord my God.
While I was fainting away,
I remembered the Lord;
And my prayer came to Thee,
Into Thy holy temple.
Those who regard vain idols
Forsake their faithfulness,
But I will sacrifice to Thee
With the voice of thanksgiving.
That which I have vowed I will pay.
Salvation is from the Lord."
Then the Lord commanded the fish, and it vom-
ited Jonah up onto the dry land. (2:1–10)

Jonah cries out in verse 3: "For Thou hast cast me into the deep." But who threw him overboard? The sailors, right? Yes, but ultimately Jonah sees God behind his circumstances. That's looking at life from God's point of view. That's insightful perspective and wisdom. Perspective like that, in the face of trials, comes only through the light of prayer. In the context of trials, James writes: "But if any of you lacks wisdom, let him ask of God, who gives to all men generously and without reproach, and it will be given to him" (1:5).

Sometimes it's difficult to see God's hand stirring the storm. There are times when we are thrown overboard and fail to recognize that He is doing the tossing. There are times, too, when we are swallowed by monstrous circumstances and held captive (Jon. 2:6), and we fail to understand that the great fish was "appointed" by God. Prayer is what gives us three-dimensional perspective to see God at work in our lives.

If the prayer in Jonah 2 teaches us anything, it instructs us that we can pray anytime, anywhere, and have confidence that no matter how suffocating and slimy our circumstances, our prayers will come before the Lord God of heaven in His holy temple (v. 7).

 ## Living Insights

In our last lesson, we studied the Book of Jonah by looking at each paragraph individually. Let's shift our focus to a biographical sketch of this prophet.

Based on your understanding of the Book of Jonah, try your hand at writing a character study of the *man* Jonah. The best way to do this is to reread the book, making notes along the way of significant demonstrations of Jonah's character. Then, gather your notes and rewrite them in a creative way. Perhaps you could write a letter of recommendation on Jonah's behalf. Maybe you'd like to write an article for a newspaper or magazine. Be as creative and imaginative as the text will allow. It will help you see this man as he really was.

_____

_____

_____

_____

_____

_____

_____

_____

_____

_____

_____

_____

_____

_____

_____

_____

🍇 *Living Insights* STUDY TWO

After an exercise like the previous character study, the next step is to compare and contrast yourself to Jonah. How do you look alongside this famous biblical character?

Using the following chart, refer to your notes from the previous Living Insights and ask yourself the following questions: In what ways are Jonah and I *alike?* In what ways are we *different?* Write your answers in the appropriate columns.

Jonah and I

Similarities _____

_____

_____

_____

Differences _____

_____

_____

_____

Chapter 12

REVIVAL! IN SPITE
OF THE EVANGELIST
Jonah 3–4

The greatest revival in the history of the world took place in a very unlikely spot on the globe. It did not occur in Scotland, as a result of John Knox's influence. Nor did it take place in England, connected with Wesley, Spurgeon, G. Campbell Morgan, or F. B. Meyer. It was not in Europe, in spite of the impact of Calvin, Luther, Zwingli, or Savonarola. Neither was it in America, although we have been blessed with the ministries of Moody, Gypsy Smith, Jonathan Edwards, Billy Sunday, and Billy Graham.

Give up? It occurred 150 miles northwest of Baghdad, near the modern city of Mosul.[1] In the vicinity of Mosul is a massive mound of earth. Beneath that mound, we are told, is the ancient tomb of the evangelist responsible for this great revival—the prophet Jonah.[2]

When we think of Jonah, we think of resistance . . . rebellion . . . retreat. But what *should* stand out in our thinking is revival, for through his preaching the entire city of Nineveh experienced a dramatic conversion.

So far, we have seen Jonah running *from* God in chapter 1 and *to* God in chapter 2. As our study opens in chapter 3, we see him running *with* God in obedience.

Jonah's Revival

After walking out on the job, Jonah returns to God with a repentant heart and is given a second chance. He embarks on the single greatest missionary effort of all time.

Physically, the journey was difficult. Jonah's trek from the eastern shore of the Mediterranean to Nineveh spanned approximately five hundred miles. Politically, making the journey worse, he was traveling in enemy territory. Spiritually, the assignment was un-

---

1. Merrill F. Unger, *Archaeology and the Old Testament* (Grand Rapids, Mich.: Zondervan Publishing House, 1970), p. 263.

2. The mound is named Nebi Yunus, Hebrew for "Prophet Jonah."

doubtedly hard for Jonah too, as he was given no latitude with regard to his message. God instructed him: "Proclaim to it the proclamation which I am going to tell you" (v. 2b).[3]

In verse 3, Nineveh is described as "an exceedingly great city, a three days' walk." As Californians designate Los Angeles to incorporate many smaller cities and suburbs, so the Hebrews designated several cities within the Nineveh metropolis.

> From that land he went forth into Assyria, and built Nineveh and Rehoboth-Ir and Calah, and Resen between Nineveh and Calah; that is the great city. (Gen. 10:11–12)

Therefore, a three days' walk through the city would be entirely reasonable.[4] During the first monotonous day of his walk, Jonah trudges the streets of this foreign metropolis—one small man calling out like a town crier against this sprawling Sodom of a city. Like a broken record, he parrots the same song: "Yet forty days and Nineveh will be overthrown . . . Yet forty days and Nineveh will be overthrown . . . Yet forty days and Nineveh will be overthrown."

Before we see the results of Jonah's monotonous cry, let's backtrack a little and pay special attention to one particular statement: "Now the word of the Lord came to Jonah the *second* time" (Jon. 3:1, emphasis added). This brief phrase reveals a great deal about God's character. He doesn't turn a deaf ear or a cold shoulder to the repentant—no matter how blatant the rebellion or which borders the runaway crosses. Like the father in the story of the Prodigal Son, God waits with open arms, fatted calf, robe, and ring to give us a second chance to serve Him.

Nineveh's Repentance

Illustrating Hebrews 4:12, the living and active Word of God cuts like a sharp, two-edged sword to pierce the hearts of the Ninevites.

> Then the people of Nineveh believed in God; and they called a fast and put on sackcloth from the

---

3. In Hebrew the *I* is the most emphatic word in the sentence. The sense of the sentence is: "*I* will give you the message to proclaim."

4. If Herodotus' definition of a day's march as seventeen miles is used, then the great city's diameter was approximately fifty miles. Leslie C. Allen, *The Books of Joel, Obadiah, Jonah, and Micah,* a volume of the *International Commentary on the Old Testament* (Grand Rapids, Mich.: William B. Eerdmans Publishing Co., 1976), p. 221.

greatest to the least of them. When the word reached
the king of Nineveh, he arose from his throne, laid
aside his robe from him, covered himself with sackcloth, and sat on the ashes. And he issued a proclamation and it said, "In Nineveh by the decree of
the king and his nobles: Do not let man, beast,
herd, or flock taste a thing. Do not let them eat or
drink water. But both man and beast must be covered with sackcloth; and let men call on God earnestly that each may turn from his wicked way and
from the violence which is in his hands. Who knows,
God may turn and relent, and withdraw His burning
anger so that we shall not perish?"

When God saw their deeds, that they turned
from their wicked way, then God relented concerning the calamity which He had declared He would
bring upon them. And He did not do it. (Jon. 3:5–10)

Even the king of Nineveh, sitting in his palace, is touched by
the carefully honed point of Jonah's message. At once, he abdicates
his high position in the ominous face of God's wrath. "His *throne*
and *royal robes* are exchanged for *sackcloth* and *ashes.*"[5] The repentance extends from "the greatest to the least"—from king to com-
moner, from man to beast.[6] As a result of repentance, God's wrath is
averted, which, as Joel states, is inherent to the Almighty's character.

"Yet even now," declares the Lord,
"Return to Me with all your heart,
And with fasting, weeping, and mourning;
And rend your heart and not your garments."
Now return to the Lord your God,
For He is gracious and compassionate,
Slow to anger, abounding in lovingkindness,
And relenting of evil. (Joel 2:12–13)

Jonah's Reaction

The heat of God's anger is cooled by the tears of Nineveh's
repentance. In His mercy He issues a death-row reprieve from their

5. Allen, *Joel, Obadiah, Jonah, and Micah,* p. 224.

6. "It was a Persian custom for animals to participate in mourning ceremonies. . . . The
gesture would impress forcibly . . . the sincerity of Nineveh's repentance." Allen, *Joel,
Obadiah, Jonah, and Micah,* p. 224.

slated execution. Jonah's reaction, however, is totally opposite. Instead of reacting like the Prodigal Son's compassionate father, Jonah responds in a way that parallels the critical older brother (see Luke 15:28).

> But it greatly displeased Jonah, and he became angry. And he prayed to the Lord and said, "Please Lord, was not this what I said while I was still in my own country? Therefore, in order to forestall this I fled to Tarshish, for I knew that Thou art a gracious and compassionate God, slow to anger and abundant in lovingkindness, and one who relents concerning calamity. Therefore now, O Lord, please take my life from me, for death is better to me than life." And the Lord said, "Do you have good reason to be angry?" (Jon. 4:1–4)

Notice carefully how God deals with the pouting prophet. No sermon. No rebuke. No argument. Just the barbed question that hung like a fishhook in his heart: "Do you have good reason to be angry?"

It is possible to have all the right theology while having a totally wrong heart. Notice how accurate, how biblical Jonah's theology is: "I knew that Thou art a gracious and compassionate God, slow to anger and abundant in lovingkindness, and one who relents concerning calamity" (v. 2b). Notice also his anger (v. 1). Right words, wrong heart.

The parables in Luke 15 picture how our hearts should respond when a sinner repents. In each incident—the lost sheep (vv. 3–7), the lost coin (vv. 8–10), the lost son (vv. 11–32)—what was lost was found, resulting in great joy (vv. 7, 10, and 32). Climactically, the father in the parable of the Prodigal Son illustrates the embracing, compassionate heart of God the Father toward a wayward child. In contrast, the critical older brother illustrates the indignant, self-righteous heart of the Pharisees and scribes (v. 2). Two portraits. A compassionate, accepting father. A critical, angry brother. You can dot every theological i and cross every exegetical t, but still be a great distance from God. As Jesus said to the hypocrites:

> "This people honors Me with their lips,
> But their heart is far away from Me." (Mark 7:6b)

The Prodigal Son's brother lived under the same roof as the father, but his heart was miles away. How about you? How close is your heart to the Father's?

God's Rebuke

Stomping off in a huff, Jonah shook the city's dust off his feet and built a box seat on a hillside to view the city's fate.

> Then Jonah went out from the city and sat east of it. There he made a shelter for himself and sat under it in the shade until he could see what would happen in the city. (Jon. 4:5)

The God of the sea, who can appoint a great fish to swallow Jonah, is also the God of the earth, who can appoint a plant to shade him.

> So the Lord God appointed a plant and it grew up over Jonah to be a shade over his head to deliver him from his discomfort. And Jonah was extremely happy about the plant. (v. 6)

Note the great emotional response that this lower level of life brought to Jonah: "And Jonah was extremely happy about the plant." With this plant, God sows an object lesson in the hard soil of Jonah's heart.

> But God appointed a worm when dawn came the next day, and it attacked the plant and it withered. And it came about when the sun came up that God appointed a scorching east wind, and the sun beat down on Jonah's head so that he became faint and begged with all his soul to die, saying, "Death is better to me than life." (vv. 7–8)

God again appoints another of his creatures—this time a worm, and this time for destruction. Not only is Jonah's shade gone, but God appoints a scorching east wind. As the sun beats down on Jonah, his joy shrivels like the leaves of the plant. Longing for death, Jonah calls out to God in despair. But there is no salve from God; only the same type of stinging question that sought him before.

> Then God said to Jonah, "Do you have good reason to be angry about the plant?" And he said, "I have good reason to be angry, even to death." (v. 9)

Jonah's answer forms a fist in God's face, but fails to ruffle the calm feathers of His patient instruction.

Then the Lord said, "You had compassion on the plant for which you did not work, and which you did not cause to grow, which came up overnight and perished overnight. And should I not have compassion on Nineveh, the great city in which there are more than 120,000 persons who do not know the difference between their right and left hand, as well as many animals?" (vv. 10–11)

God's words pour into Jonah's soul like salt into sun-scorched blisters. With a light hand but a sharp hoe, God cultivates the object lesson He planted in Jonah's heart. Essentially, God puts His arm around Jonah and seems to be saying, "Let's talk about this concern you had for the plant, Jonah."

> "What did it really mean to you? Your attachment to it could not be very deep, for it was here one day and *gone the next*. Your concern was dictated by self-interest, not by a genuine love. You never had for it the devotion of the gardener. If you feel as badly as you do, what would you expect a gardener to feel like, who tended a plant and watched it grow only to see it wither and die, poor thing? And this is how I feel about Nineveh, only much more so. All those people, all those animals—I made them, I have cherished them all these years. Nineveh has cost me no end of effort, and they mean the world to me. Your pain is nothing to mine when I contemplate their destruction."[7]

With the object lesson deeply rooted in Jonah's heart, the embittered prophet stands silent before the court of heaven—a mute testimony to the truth of God's argument. And thus we leave Jonah —never to hear his voice in the Scriptures again.

 Living Insights

Jonah's value scale was so unbalanced . . . his vision, so near-sighted . . . his life, so small. An insignificant, soulless plant meant

---

7. Allen, *Joel, Obadiah, Jonah, and Micah,* p. 234.

more to him than anything on earth. The lesson of the book is that Jonah was more concerned about Jonah than he was about Nineveh.

What's the lesson of your life? Are you more concerned with building shelters and raising plants—more concerned about creature comforts and selfish living—than the deep, spiritual needs of people? On a one-to-ten scale—one being your concern for your own physical comfort and ten being your concern for the spiritual needs of others—how would you evaluate yourself?

1 2 3 4 5 6 7 8 9 10

What needs to take place in your life to move that number up? (see Phil. 2:3–8)

_____

_____

Are there some plants in your life that need to be removed so you can see your Nineveh? Describe each one in detail.

The Plant

_____

_____

_____

The Root

_____

_____

_____

The Fruit

_____

_____

_____

_____

Living Insights

No review of these character studies would be complete without a look at the changes in our lives that result. Living Insights are designed with application in mind. Let's look back over the most meaningful ones we learned.

Look through your study guide, and pick one meaningful application from each lesson.

Old Testament Characters

1. Samson: A He-Man with a She-Weakness _____

_____

2. Samson: How the Mighty Are Fallen! _____

_____

3. Abigail: A Woman of Wisdom _____

_____

4. Absalom: The Rebel Prince Charming _____

_____

5. Rehoboam: The Reckless Phony _____

_____

6. Naaman and Gehazi: Characters in Contrast _____

_____

7. Jabez: Disabled but Not Disqualified _____

_____

8. Uzziah: The King Who Became a Leper _____

_____

9. From Captive to Queen: An Adoption Story _____

_____

10. Mr. Jones, Meet Mr. Jonah _____

_____

BOOKS FOR
PROBING FURTHER

In his essay *Reflections in Westminster Abbey*, seventeenth-century writer Joseph Addison records his thoughts on a stroll through the church and burial place of Britain's famous.

> When I look upon the tombs of the great, every emotion of envy dies in me. When I read the epitaphs of the beautiful, every inordinate desire goes out. When I meet with the grief of parents upon a tombstone, my heart melts with compassion. When I see the tomb of the parents themselves, I consider the vanity of grieving for those whom we must quickly follow. When I see kings lying by those who deposed them, when I consider rival wits placed side by side, or the holy men that divided the world with their contests and disputes, I reflect with sorrow and astonishment on the little competitions, factions, and debates of mankind. When I read the several dates of the tombs, of some that died yesterday, and some six hundred years ago, I consider that great day when we shall all of us be contemporaries, and make our appearance together.[1]

Death is the common denominator of all mankind. And epitaphs, like file folder tabs, serve to summarize our lives in the fewest words possible. The titles to our studies on *Old Testament Characters* have summarily reduced their lives, like epitaphs, for convenient mental reference.

Samson: How the Mighty Are Fallen!
Abigail: A Woman of Wisdom
Absalom: The Rebel Prince Charming
Rehoboam: The Reckless Phony
Naaman and Gehazi: Characters in Contrast

---

1. As quoted in *The Original McGuffey's: The Fourth Eclectic Reader*, ed. Jean Morton (Milford, Mich.: Mott Media, 1982), pp. 401–2.

Jabez: Disabled but Not Disqualified
Uzziah: The King Who Became a Leper
Esther: From Captive to Queen
Jonah: The Prodigal Preacher

When we think of specific biblical characters, certain associations come immediately to mind. For example, what association do you make when you think of the apostle John? Probably the words *the disciple whom Jesus loved* pop into your mind. When you think of Judas, does the word *traitor* burn before your eyes? How about Peter? Mary and Martha? The rich young ruler? The Prodigal Son?

The word or words that come immediately to mind form the premise of that person's life . . . what that person stood for . . . what that person's life meant. What words or phrases come to mind when people think of your life? What images flash on their mental screens?

Hopefully, you have benefited from our brief walk through the cemetery where these Old Testament characters are buried. There's nothing like the cold granite reality that death forces us to touch— the reality that one day each of us will be there too. Each with a tombstone. Each with an epitaph etched in eternity.

The tombstones of most of our Old Testament characters are splotched with sin. Lust, greed, pride, ambition, deception, bitterness, and rebellion crawl over the headstones like lichen. Their epitaphs contain a warning to keep your life from ending up the same way. Listed below are several books that I think will give you an epitaph that will stand the test of eternity.

Petersen, J. Allen. *The Myth of the Greener Grass.* Wheaton, Ill.: Tyndale House Publishers, 1983. Like Delilah enticing Samson, the flame of adultery may first appear warm and comforting, but in the final analysis, it sears and scars its participants. Many a marriage has been reduced to ashes because of infidelity. Is there hope for a relationship charred by adultery? Can there be forgiveness? Can oneness be restored? The author deals with these difficult questions in the light of both modern psychology and the truth of God's Word. With sensitivity and insight he unearths the root causes of the problem, the warning signs of a deteriorating marriage, and ways to "affair-proof" a healthy marriage.

Schaeffer, Edith. *A Way of Seeing.* Old Tappan, N.J.: Fleming H. Revell Co., 1977. One of the reasons some of the Old Testament characters got into trouble on such a catastrophic scale was the presence of blind spots. If they had developed a different way of seeing—more sensitive, more responsive—much pain could have been averted. A *Way of Seeing* will open up a new way of looking at life in general, and at *your* life in particular. In this personal kaleidoscope the author gives us vivid glimpses of daily life, illuminating such concepts as trust, faith, security, death, love, and fear. These pieces were first written for the magazine *Christianity Today* and later compiled into a book due to enthusiastic reader response.

Swindoll, Charles R. *Strike the Original Match.* Portland, Oreg.: Multnomah Press, 1980. Abigail was an example of a woman who tried faithfully to hold her marriage together. No easy task, for building a good marriage is a lot like building a fine home. The architect must be consulted, a solid foundation poured, and the best material used. And, no matter how fine a finished product, termites can always destroy it. Recognizing that the idea of marriage originated with God, this book calls for a fresh and detailed look at His original blueprint and offers practical, positive advice.

White, John. *Eros Defiled: The Christian and Sexual Sin.* Downers Grove, Ill.: InterVarsity Press, 1978. In spite of Samson's strength, he succumbed to one weakness—lust. Similarly, sexual sin has destroyed many a strong person, strong marriage, strong family, strong church. With a Christlike mixture of compassion and conviction—"grace and truth"—Dr. White speaks openly about the Christian and sexual sin.

———. *The Fight.* Downers Grove, Ill.: InterVarsity Press, 1978. The epitaphs of our Old Testament characters, by and large, look like a graveyard of defeated people. Rehoboam was defeated by ambition, Gehazi by greed, Uzziah by pride. Only a few—Abigail, Naaman, Jabez, Esther—triumphed in their faith. The life of faith is a constant struggle with "the world, the flesh, and the devil." There *is* joy and triumph in the Christian life, but it is often preceded by and mysteriously intertwined with struggle. White takes us through the basic areas of Christian living that we wrestle with throughout our lives: faith, prayer, temptation, evangelism, guidance, Bible study, fellowship, work. Applied, this book can help build a warmly remembered epitaph that will stand the tests of both time and eternity.

————. *Parents in Pain.* Downers Grove, Ill.: InterVarsity Press, 1979. Parental pain is almost universal to one degree or another. Even Israel's greatest king, David, experienced great pain with his son Absalom. Undoubtedly, many parents cannot cope with the problems they must face with their children—rebellion, runaways, substance abuse, homosexuality, even suicide. In this unique book, the author doesn't give pat prescriptions to straighten out your child. Rather, he helps *you,* as a parent, deal with your sense of guilt, frustration, anger, and inadequacy.

Some of the books listed here may be out-of-print and available only through a library. All of these works are recommended reading only. With the exception of books by Charles R. Swindoll, none of them are available through Insight for Living. If you wish to obtain some of these suggested readings, please contact your local Christian bookstore.

ACKNOWLEDGMENTS

Insight for Living is grateful for permission to quote from the following source:

Carmichael, Amy. *Toward Jerusalem*. Fort Washington, Pa.: Christian Literature Crusade, 1961; London, England: Society for Promoting Christian Knowledge, 1950.

ORDERING INFORMATION

Cassette Tapes and Study Guide

This Bible study guide was designed to be used independently or in conjunction with the broadcast of Chuck Swindoll's taped messages on the topic listed below. If you would like to order cassette tapes or further copies of this study guide, please see the information given below and the order forms provided at the back of this guide.

OLD TESTAMENT CHARACTERS

Scriptural character studies never fail to encourage us in our pilgrimage. That is one of the reasons God included snapshots of so many people in His Book. He wants us to see His truth reflected in all these lives—even in the most obscure and unfamiliar individuals.

These messages will introduce ten Old Testament personalities to you. As they are unveiled, the end goal is that you will receive helpful perspective and wisdom, which will result in greater stability, a stronger commitment to biblical principles, and a broader awareness of how God works in our lives today.

			Calif.*	U.S.	B.C.*	Canada*
OTC	SG	Study Guide	$ 4.18	$ 3.95	$ 5.08	$ 5.08
OTC	CS	Cassette series, includes album cover	36.57	34.50	49.44	46.81
OTC	1–6	Individual cassettes, include messages A and B	5.30	5.00	7.18	6.79

*These prices already include the following charges: for delivery in **California**, 6% sales tax; Canada, 7% postage and handling; **British Columbia**, 6% British Columbia sales tax (on tapes only) and 7% postage and handling. The prices are subject to change without notice.

OTC 1-A: *Samson: A He-Man with a She-Weakness*—Judges 13–15
     B: *Samson: How the Mighty Are Fallen!*—Judges 16:4–31

OTC 2-A: *Abigail: A Woman of Wisdom*—1 Samuel 25
     B: *Absalom: The Rebel Prince Charming*—2 Samuel 13–18

OTC 3-A: *Rehoboam: The Reckless Phony*—1 Kings 11–14
     B: *Naaman and Gehazi: Characters in Contrast*—2 Kings 5

OTC 4-A: *Jabez: Disabled but Not Disqualified*—1 Chronicles 4:9–10
     B: *Uzziah: The King Who Became a Leper*—2 Chronicles 26
OTC 5-A: *From Captive to Queen: An Adoption Story*—Romans 8,
       Galatians 4, Esther
     B: *Mr. Jones, Meet Mr. Jonah*—Jonah
OTC 6-A: *The Prodigal Preacher*—Jonah 1–2
     B: *Revival! In Spite of the Evangelist*—Jonah 3–4

How to Order by Mail

Simply mark on the order form whether you want the series or individual tapes. Mail the form with your payment to the appropriate address listed below. We will process your order as promptly as we can.

United States: Mail your order to the Sales Department at Insight for Living, Post Office Box 4444, Fullerton, California 92634. If you wish your order to be shipped first-class for faster delivery, add 10 percent of the total order amount. Otherwise, please allow four to six weeks for delivery by fourth-class mail. We accept personal checks, money orders, Visa, or MasterCard in payment for materials. Unfortunately, we are unable to offer invoicing or COD orders.

Canada: Mail your order to Insight for Living Ministries, Post Office Box 2510, Vancouver, British Columbia V6B 3W7. Allow approximately four weeks for delivery. We accept personal checks, money orders, Visa, or MasterCard in payment for materials. Unfortunately, we are unable to offer invoicing or COD orders.

Australia, New Zealand, or Papua New Guinea: Mail your order to Insight for Living, Inc., GPO Box 2823 EE, Melbourne, Victoria 3001, Australia. Please allow six to ten weeks for delivery by surface mail. If you would like your order sent airmail, the delivery time may be reduced. Using the United States price as a base, add postage costs—surface or airmail—to the amount of your order. Please use the chart that follows to determine correct postage. Due to fluctuating currency rates, we can accept only personal checks made payable in U.S. funds, international money orders, Visa, or MasterCard in payment for materials.

Overseas: Other overseas residents should mail their orders to our United States office. Please allow six to ten weeks for delivery by surface mail. If you would like your order sent airmail, the delivery time may be reduced. Using the United States price as a base, add postage costs—surface or airmail—to the amount of your order. Please use the chart that follows to determine correct postage. Due to fluctuating currency rates, we can accept only personal checks made payable in U.S. funds, international money orders, Visa, or MasterCard in payment for materials.

Type of Postage	Postage Cost
Surface	10% of total order
Airmail	25% of total order

For Faster Service, Order by Telephone or FAX

For Visa or MasterCard orders, you are welcome to use one of our toll-free numbers between the hours of 8:00 A.M. and 4:30 P.M., Pacific time, Monday through Friday, or our FAX numbers. The numbers to use from anywhere in the United States are **1-800-772-8888** or FAX (714) 773-0932. To order from Canada, call our Vancouver office using **1-800-663-7639** or FAX (604) 596-2975. Vancouver residents, call (604) 596-2910. Australian residents should phone (03) 872-4606. From overseas, call our Sales Department at (714) 870-9161 in the United States.

Our Guarantee

Our cassettes are guaranteed for ninety days against faulty performance or breakage due to a defect in the tape. For best results, please be sure your tape recorder is in good operating condition and is cleaned regularly.

Note: To cover processing and handling, there is a $10 fee for *any* returned check.

Order Form

OTC CS represents the entire *Old Testament Characters* series in a special album cover, while OTC 1–6 are the individual tapes included in the series. OTC SG represents this study guide, should you desire to order further copies.

Item	Calif.*	U.S.	B.C.*	Canada*	Quantity	Amount
		Unit Price				
OTC CS	$36.57	$34.50	$49.44	$46.81		$
OTC 1	5.30	5.00	7.18	6.79		
OTC 2	5.30	5.00	7.18	6.79		
OTC 3	5.30	5.00	7.18	6.79		
OTC 4	5.30	5.00	7.18	6.79		
OTC 5	5.30	5.00	7.18	6.79		
OTC 6	5.30	5.00	7.18	6.79		
OTC SG	4.18	3.95	5.08	5.08		
					Subtotal	
					Overseas Residents *Pay U.S. price plus 10% surface postage or 25% airmail. Also, see "How to Order by Mail."*	
					U.S. First-Class Shipping *For faster delivery, add 10% for postage and handling.*	
					Gift to Insight for Living *Tax-deductible in the United States and Canada.*	
					Total Amount Due *Please do not send cash.*	$

If there is a balance: ☐ apply it as a donation ☐ please refund
*These prices already include applicable taxes and shipping costs.

Payment by: ☐ Check or money order made payable to Insight for Living or

☐ Credit card (circle one): Visa MasterCard Number _____

Expiration Date _____ Signature _____
We cannot process your credit card purchase without your signature.

Name _____

Address _____

City _____ State/Province _____

Zip/Postal Code _____ Country _____

Telephone ( ) _____ Radio Station ___ ___ ___ ___
If questions arise concerning your order, we may need to contact you.

Mail this order form to the Sales Department at one of these addresses:
Insight for Living, Post Office Box 4444, Fullerton, CA 92634
Insight for Living Ministries, Post Office Box 2510, Vancouver, BC, Canada V6B 3W7
Insight for Living, Inc., GPO Box 2823 EE, Melbourne, VIC 3001, Australia

Order Form

OTC CS represents the entire *Old Testament Characters* series in a special album cover, while OTC 1–6 are the individual tapes included in the series. OTC SG represents this study guide, should you desire to order further copies.

Item	Calif.*	U.S.	B.C.*	Canada*	Quantity	Amount
OTC CS	$36.57	$34.50	$49.44	$46.81		$
OTC 1	5.30	5.00	7.18	6.79		
OTC 2	5.30	5.00	7.18	6.79		
OTC 3	5.30	5.00	7.18	6.79		
OTC 4	5.30	5.00	7.18	6.79		
OTC 5	5.30	5.00	7.18	6.79		
OTC 6	5.30	5.00	7.18	6.79		
OTC SG	4.18	3.95	5.08	5.08		
					Subtotal	
	Overseas Residents *Pay U.S. price plus 10% surface postage or 25% airmail. Also, see "How to Order by Mail."*					
	U.S. First-Class Shipping *For faster delivery, add 10% for postage and handling.*					
	Gift to Insight for Living *Tax-deductible in the United States and Canada.*					
	Total Amount Due *Please do not send cash.*					$

Unit Price heading spans Calif.*, U.S., B.C.*, and Canada* columns.

If there is a balance: ☐ apply it as a donation ☐ please refund
*These prices already include applicable taxes and shipping costs.

Payment by: ☐ Check or money order made payable to Insight for Living or

☐ Credit card (circle one): Visa MasterCard Number _____

Expiration Date _____ Signature _____
We cannot process your credit card purchase without your signature.

Name _____

Address _____

City _____ State/Province _____

Zip/Postal Code _____ Country _____

Telephone (____) _____ Radio Station ___ ___ ___ ___
If questions arise concerning your order, we may need to contact you.

Mail this order form to the Sales Department at one of these addresses:
Insight for Living, Post Office Box 4444, Fullerton, CA 92634
Insight for Living Ministries, Post Office Box 2510, Vancouver, BC, Canada V6B 3W7
Insight for Living, Inc., GPO Box 2823 EE, Melbourne, VIC 3001, Australia

Order Form

OTC CS represents the entire *Old Testament Characters* series in a special album cover, while OTC 1–6 are the individual tapes included in the series. OTC SG represents this study guide, should you desire to order further copies.

Item	Calif.*	U.S.	B.C.*	Canada*	Quantity	Amount
		Unit Price				
OTC CS	$36.57	$34.50	$49.44	$46.81		$
OTC 1	5.30	5.00	7.18	6.79		
OTC 2	5.30	5.00	7.18	6.79		
OTC 3	5.30	5.00	7.18	6.79		
OTC 4	5.30	5.00	7.18	6.79		
OTC 5	5.30	5.00	7.18	6.79		
OTC 6	5.30	5.00	7.18	6.79		
OTC SG	4.18	3.95	5.08	5.08		
					Subtotal	
	Overseas Residents *Pay U.S. price plus 10% surface postage or 25% airmail. Also, see "How to Order by Mail."*					
	U.S. First-Class Shipping *For faster delivery, add 10% for postage and handling.*					
	Gift to Insight for Living *Tax-deductible in the United States and Canada.*					
	Total Amount Due *Please do not send cash.*					$

If there is a balance: ☐ apply it as a donation ☐ please refund
*These prices already include applicable taxes and shipping costs.

Payment by: ☐ Check or money order made payable to Insight for Living or

☐ Credit card (circle one): Visa   MasterCard   Number _____

Expiration Date _____ Signature _____
We cannot process your credit card purchase without your signature.

Name _____

Address _____

City _____ State/Province _____

Zip/Postal Code _____ Country _____

Telephone ( ) _____ Radio Station ___ ___ ___ ___
If questions arise concerning your order, we may need to contact you.

Mail this order form to the Sales Department at one of these addresses:
Insight for Living, Post Office Box 4444, Fullerton, CA 92634
Insight for Living Ministries, Post Office Box 2510, Vancouver, BC, Canada V6B 3W7
Insight for Living, Inc., GPO Box 2823 EE, Melbourne, VIC 3001, Australia